JOURNAL

OF THE

SUTLEJ CAMPAIGN OF 1845-6,

AND ALSO OF

LORD HARDINGE'S TOUR

IN

THE FOLLOWING WINTER.

BY

JAMES COLEY, M.A.,

CHAPLAIN TO THE HONOURABLE EAST INDIA COMPANY.

The Naval & Military Press Ltd

in association with

The National Army Museum, London

Published jointly by

The Naval & Military Press Ltd
Unit 10 Ridgewood Industrial Park,
Uckfield, East Sussex,
TN22 5QE England

Tel: +44 (0) 1825 749494
Fax: +44 (0) 1825 765701

www.naval-military-press.com
www.military-genealogy.com
www.militarymaproom.com

and

The National Army Museum, London
www.national-army-museum.ac.uk

In reprinting in facsimile from the original, any imperfections are inevitably reproduced and the quality may fall short of modern type and cartographic standards.

INTRODUCTION.

I WAS on leave at Simla, in the autumn of 1845, having been driven there by a dangerous illness at Cánpoor, and was rapidly recovering my health in that delightful sanatarium, when I was appointed Chaplain to the Governor-General, Sir Henry Hardinge, then on a tour through the Upper Provinces. I felt that my new position would be one of peculiar responsibility, and I prayed and resolved earnestly to be faithful in my sacred ministry, whatever the people might be, whom I was about to join.

The First Part of this Journal was written between December 3, 1845, and March 23, 1846; the greater portion of which period was immortalized by the memorable Sutlej campaign. I did not write for publication, or what I have written would have been less imperfect than it is. But I have since been induced to think, that to offer my Journal, such as it is, to the perusal of others, may, perhaps, be of some use; that it may be the means of communicating some information relative to that eventful time, and not obtainable from other sources, that will be of interest, especially to those who care for such intelligence, as I, from the nature of my office, might be supposed likely to give. Everyone, that was eye-witness of any of the scenes of that period, would, of course, make his own observations for himself, and therefore have a separate tale to tell. I, also, had my own peculiar sphere of observation, more limited, indeed, in some respects, but at the same time one, that in other respects was calculated to give me an advantage. In a picturesque country, different travellers fix their eyes upon different objects; in an engaging book, different readers are struck by different passages. So, in a campaign, the soldier gathers materials for one narrative, the civilian for another, the minister of religion for another. My acquaintance with the details of the battles and those circumstances, upon which the military writer would mainly dwell, was not sufficiently accurate to enable me to note them down; and, if it had been, I should have suppressed them in sending my Journal to the press, because they have already been given to the world by others much more competent to relate them, than myself. What therefore will distinguish my brief record is this; that in addition to a cursory allusion to such occurrences and scenes as might attract the notice of a general observer, I have mentioned things, the cognisance of which either fell exclusively within my sphere of duty, or would probably be taken but by very few, or which from the nature of my vocation or opinions, or bent of mind, pressed themselves upon my attention; and moreover I have given free and unreserved expression to such religious thoughts and reflections, as could not but arise in a Christian's breast, or at least arose in mine, on various occasions. My only regret is, that such reflections were not more full and frequent than they were.

I ought to say, that I have altered the original Journal in some places, where a re-perusal of it or subsequent experience or information may have suggested the necessity of so doing; that I have omitted many notes of a private and uninteresting kind; and that here and there I have appended remarks entirely new, the posterior date of which will speak for itself. I must add, that the First Part of the Journal was originally printed, nearly in its present state, in the *Calcutta Christian Intelligencer*. I have made some omissions and some alterations, and added some notes.

The Second Part of the Journal, or that written during the tour in the cold weather of 1846-7, now published for the first time, describes more tranquil scenes, and circumstances more congenial to the spirit of a "minister of God and steward of the mysteries of Christ," wounded and vexed though still this spirit too often was by many objects and causes of offence; inasmuch as it exhibits, in the blessings attendant upon British rule and government, a refreshing contrast to the miserable consequences of anarchy and political and moral profligacy, as well as to those horrors of warfare and bloodshed, which are so frequently necessary for the introduction of peace and the establishment of civil and social order.

I do not profess an exact acquaintance with civil statistics and such matters; and this must be my apology, should any inaccuracies be detected in any statements I have made or *on dits* I have recorded.

Oriental words I have written in English characters and as they are, or ought to be, pronounced in English: for, if I had written them in Oriental characters, they would not have been understood by the generality of English readers; and, if I had merely Anglicised the Oriental letters, the words would have been mispronounced. An accent (') placed over a vowel signifies that the pronunciation is broad, or as of the same vowel in French. In " Proposals for a Missionary

Alphabet" by Professor Max Müller, and in " Das allgemeine linguistische Alphabet" by Dr. Lepsius, we have the promise of some uniform system of orthography for Oriental names in Occidental characters; and truly it is a great desideratum, on the supposition of its unanimous adoption by Missionaries; but yet I fear that the generality of readers would never take the pains to learn and understand it.

J. C.

# JOURNAL

OF THE

SUTLEJ CAMPAIGN OF 1845-6.

PART I.

§ 1. DEPARTURE FROM UMBALLA.

DEC. 3*rd*, 1845.—I joined the Governor-General's Camp at Umballa. I have a single-poled tent next above the Commissariat-Officer's in the Governor-General's street: the food for the soul and the food for the body being, I suppose, thought best in juxta-position, as the one cannot go on without the other; though for some reasons I should have thought it a more correct arrangement, if they had been placed *opposite* each other. My tents are provided for me by Government free of all expense, which is a great advantage, but nothing more than is due to an Assistant Chaplain. A camp like this is a novel spectacle to me; and to belong to it, quite a new life. Pitched on good ground and with the main street as smooth as a bowling-green, it is an exceedingly pretty sight. I believe I am an entire stranger to all the members of the camp, except the Quarter-Master, whom I recollect at Cánpoor.

4th.—I had the honour for the first time of dining with the Governor-General. A very large party in two splendid tents, the one serving for drawing-room, the other for dining-room. No grace was said: owing perhaps to the noise and confusion of so large a party sitting down. After dinner I was introduced to the Governor-General by Mr. Currie, Secretary to Government. The Seekhs are talked about; but the general opinion seems to be, that there is not much probability of a war. The Governor-General's exquisite band played during dinner.

5th.—We marched out of Umballa and halted on the other side of the river Guggur, a distance of about six miles.

6th.—(Sunday.)—I am glad to hear that the

Governor-General always halts on Sundays. We halted to-day. I had prepared for Divine Service; and at 10 o'clock the Governor-General sent me word that he wished Divine Service to be held in his tent at 11. I found one of the durbár-tents (*a*) very suitably arranged for the purpose: chairs on each side, a table and chair at one end for the Governor-General and a table and chair at the other end for me, which I think is at least quite as good a substitute for a *pulpitum*, as the military apparatus of a drum-head or what may be called a " drum ecclesiastic." I read the Morning Prayer and Litany and, having retired to exchange the surplice for the gown, discoursed upon Tit. ii. 11, 12, 13, 14. As there is no psalmody to fill up the interval, it is my intention to read the Communion-service only on those occasions, when the Sacrament of the Lord's Supper is administered. For the same reason I shall discontinue the change of robes and wear my surplice during the sermon. As I have delivered a sermon in my gown once,

(*a*) *Durbár*, a court or hall of audience.

I trust the congregation will not take alarm. The congregation was small: this might possibly be owing to the shortness of the notice given. There was no more Divine Service to-day in the Governor-General's tent; but I availed myself of another tent for the purpose of evening, or rather afternoon, Service and sent round a notice to the members of the camp; very few however attended. I dined with the Governor-General. I have had melancholy occasion to perceive that no distinction of days is observed by most of the company as to *conversation;* and the sacredness of this day adds to the grief I feel at witnessing the light and jocular manner in which some Officers speak of the vicious habits of soldiers. So true is the Scripture, "Fools make a mock at sin."

8th.—Rájpoora. A march of ten miles and a very uninteresting road.

9th.—Patarsee, eight and a half miles.

10th.—Sirhind, nine miles. This is a place of ruins. I saw one fine ruin, that of a musjid (*b*).

(*b*) *Musjid,* a mosque.

DEPARTURE FROM UMBALLA.

Ahmad Sháh, the Affghán Governor of Lahore, defeated the Seekhs here in the year 1762. The following year the Seekhs sacked Sirhind and reduced it to the ruin it is now and killed the Governor, Zyne Khán. One of the most perfect vestiges of Mahommedan dominion in this part of the country is the *cóss-minár*, or large conical pillar erected along the road-side at the distance of every cóss, (c) corresponding to our mile-stone. I understand that these cóss-minárs extended from Delhi to Lahore. The mornings are very cold and the early riding exercise very delightful. I ride alone and live alone all day; but indeed I cannot call it solitude, so long as I have my books to read and my Lord to commune with. If I were deprived of this independence, I should be much more lonely; to be dependant on the world for happiness, "this, this is solitude, this is to be alone."

(c) *Cóss*, 2 English miles.

§ 2. COMMENCEMENT OF THE CAMPAIGN.

11th.—Lushkur Khán ki Sarái, 11 miles.—Here the road parts: one branch takes to Loodiána, the other to Ferozepoor; this however to Ferozepoor being, I understand, a short cut rather than a regular road. The Governor-General went over to Loodiána in his carriage, to inspect the force there, and returned in the afternoon. He has a palanquin-carriage drawn by four mules, which is very well adapted for the primitive roads in this part of the country: they are anything but carriage-roads and in many places mere sandy lanes.

13th.—The order was given, as usual, to halt on Sunday; but in the course of the day intelligence being brought to the Governor-General that the Seekhs had crossed the Sutlej, subsequent orders were issued to march to-morrow morning.

COMMENCEMENT OF THE CAMPAIGN.

The surprise in camp is great: for, though rumours of their hostile intentions have been long prevailing and growing louder and louder, it was not expected that the Seekhs would carry their arrogant menace into execution; it was looked upon as the mere bravado of a blustering threat, which would pass off without harm, as similar demonstrations had done in 1843 and '44. It seems however to be anticipated that they will not give us much trouble, nor keep their ground long, and will soon have cause to repent of their folly. Their attitude, till now, has been something like that of the Goths in Illyricum, hovering on the borders of the western Empire and ready to embrace the opportunity of Theodosius' death for an incursion; or like that of the Saracens, at the outset of their career, rushing from the Arabian desert and threatening Syria with an invasion, but advancing only to retire; it now remains to be seen, whether the comparison will hold much farther or not: whether these infuriated barbarians will still go on, as they boast, and accomplish their design and bring over our dominions a tempest of desolation like that, which the Goths carried into the western Empire in the beginning of the 5th century and the Saracens into the eastern in the beginning of the 7th. That we, as a nation, deserve such a chastisement, there can be no doubt; yet nevertheless μὴ γένοιτο.

14th.—(Sunday.)—*Gunguss*, 10 miles.—This has been an unusual sabbath to me; but, so far as the marching is concerned, the case is one of evident and undoubted necessity, and "the Son of man is Lord also of the sabbath." There has been no Divine Service, nor any thing outward to remind one of the day. All is excitement and anxiety about what is to happen. In the midst of all which however I hope that private and secret prayers will not be forgotten, and that fervent supplications will go up to the throne of grace from him and for him, who occupies the most responsible position in the direction of our affairs, that the Divine guidance and blessing may be vouchsafed to all his councils at this important crisis. I dined with the Governor-General: horses and swords were the principal topics of discourse, a little relief to which I experienced in conversing with one of the company about Bishop Middleton on the Greek Article, of which work he truly observed, that it answers many of the objections of infidels.(^d)

15th.—*Luttálah*, 12½ miles.—At this place the Governor-General's camp has been joined by that of Sir Hugh Gough, the Commander-in-Chief, who has come from Umballa by forced marches. Every day now assumes a more military aspect. The ladies, who were marching with the camp in anticipation of a peaceful and delightful tour, have been very prudently required to leave it and retire to Umballa, Meerut, and other stations out of the way.

(^d) Upon the whole however throughout the campaign it was remarkable how much *general* conversation was sustained, and with what affability and readiness the Governor-General himself, as well as others, discoursed in the evening upon a variety of topics quite unconnected with the all-absorbing subject of the day.

16*th.*—*Wudnee*, 30 miles.—I have only one horse, though scarcely large enough to be dignified with the name; but he seems to be an indefatigable creature : he has carried me this long march at a good pace, and appears none the worse for it. At a village on the road called *Busseah* a concentration of our forces took place. Thence we marched all together to Wudnee. This is a new and interesting sight to me, the marching of an army. I feel a sort of enthusiasm in beholding it, and in reflecting, that it is not an aggressive army fired with blood-thirstiness and the lust of conquest and plunder, but a Christian army going forth in a holy cause, for the assertion of justice between nation and nation, and for the defence of our country, our rights, and our Sovereign against the unprovoked attack of an insolent and lawless enemy. The Governor-General has, I believe, issued a proclamation, calling upon all in the protected Seekh states, and all, indeed, on either side of the river, that will, to place themselves under British protection, and warning them against the consequences of refusal. The people of this village have manifested that they are hostile to us, and that they are under Seekh influence, and acknowledge no other protection than that of Lahore.

On our arrival this morning, the fort was manned with armed Seekhs, who made what demonstration they could. They fired with their match-locks at Count Oriolo, but missed him. Count Oriolo is one of the staff of Prince Waldemar, who has attached himself to the Governor-General's suite in expectation of witnessing an engagement between the British and Seekh forces. He is attended by another count, and by a German surgeon. When I arrived, not a single tent was visible, and no one could tell me where the Governor-General's party was to be found. In this perplexity I rode round and round for about an hour, till my eye was caught by something like a table and chair in the corner of a *tope*, or small grove of trees, and then by the Governor-General and Commander-in-Chief and a few others, with some parchments before them, engaged in grave consultation. Near this spot our tents were pitched in process of time, most of us having to wait till the afternoon. In the course of my wanderings this morning, I passed twice under the fort, and attempted once to enter, but the gate was shut, and a man from inside told me there was no admission. This I did in perfect ignorance of the state of things. The villagers looked sour and surly; nor did I like the appearance of the men with their match-locks at the top of the fort. I asked them where the Lord Sáhib (*e*) was; in answer to which they growled something, the only word of which I could comprehend was " Farungee."(*f*) They did not fire at me, though I was quite alone; and had it been an hour or two earlier, I might have encountered the same sort of salutation as Count Oriolo, and, perhaps, not have escaped so well.

(*e*) The name, by which the natives call the Governor-General.

(*f*) Commonly pronounced *faringee:* the *g* is hard. The word means an European.

COMMENCEMENT OF THE CAMPAIGN. 13

My luggage comes up now-a-days about nightfall. I have, therefore, a good appetite by the time of its arrival, not however without having first gone through the diversion of a head-ache during the heat of the day, which is with me the invariable effect of hunger. I have no conveyance for my luggage but a hackery, or bullock-cart, which has no chance against these long marches and heavy roads. Had I been an experienced campaigner, I should have done what I could at Umballa to procure camels; but it is too late now for correcting such mistakes as these: so I must be contented with my present slow team of three oxen and one buffalo, and learn from them a lesson of patience, for I think they are the most patient of all beasts.

17*th.—Chirruk*, 10 miles.—We know nothing of what is going on at Ferozepoor, the dâk (*g*) communication having been cut off by the Seekhs. But I believe, that, when the Governor-General last heard from Sir J. Littler, the General com-

(*g*) Post.

manding the Ferozepoor force, Sir John assured him, that he entertained no fear whatever about himself, and was confident that he should be able to defend his post.

§ 3. BATTLE OF MOODKEE.

18th.—Moodkee.—I saw no Quarter-master's order-book to-day, and therefore do not know the distance of the march, but I should say about twenty miles. We had a long time to wait for our tents. This place has nothing to distinguish it, except the memorable event which has occurred to-day in its neighbourhood: it is a common mud village. Before we arrived here, a messenger met us on the road to announce, that the enemy was advancing towards us. The army was ordered to halt and form for battle. We were all in good spirits and in breathless expectation: I felt the eagerness of a soldier. I should have had a good view of the commencement of the combat, as the Governor-General and Staff were in front. But, shortly after, another message being brought to inform us that it was a false alarm, the army was ordered to march. On our arrival at the village, we heard that the Seekh army was within five miles of us; but some said that they did not believe one word of the report. Many have thought all along, that the Seekhs would run away as soon as ever they heard of the approach of our army; but Major Broadfoot's opinion has been, that the probabilities were in favour of a battle. The villagers here refusing supplies, the village was sacked. Before our arrival, an Officer of the name of Biddulph, with four Seepáhees, and one Náyak([h]), who were marching alone to Ferozepoor, apparently unconscious of the state of affairs, were fallen upon and taken prisoners and confined in the fort, together with their horses and camels; and Captain B. was afterwards carried off no one knows where. This story I heard related by one of the four Seepáhees, who seemed to be in a dreadful fright. The Governor-General was sitting under a tree with a table and official papers and boxes before

([h]) Corporal in a native regiment.

him, till his tent was ready. He is an old soldier, and therefore accustomed to the rough work of such times as these. During the march I have seen him sit on the ground under a tree, waiting for the troops to come up. It is the same for all, from the lowest to the highest. None of us are allowed more than one tent, as of course no tents can be sent on a-head; and many are obliged to *double up*. But there is a diverting excitement, which prevents such inconveniences from being felt as hardships. I do not know what they may be to the lady, whom I observed with astonishment here this morning on horseback, in the midst of the troops, with no bonnet nor hat on. Who she is, or what brings her here, I cannot imagine. There is a large pool here, which was quite a picturesque sight when filled with soldiers, who rushed into it up to their middles the moment they arrived, to quench their thirst. Most of them looked fagged and exhausted, and some of the Europeans as if readier for the hospital than for the field. This circumstance renders the victory of to-day still more wonderful, and must force a religious mind to acknowledge, that in the midst of our weakness the strength of the Lord of Hosts has been signally illustrated.

We were all quiet in our tents, anticipating that, when we arrived at Ferozepoor, we should join Sir J. Littler's force and then fall upon the enemy, or, if they had retired across the river, pursue them into the Punjáb; nothing was seen or heard of them, except another report, that they were close upon us, which however was discredited as having no foundation, and was even treated with ridicule and contempt by some, who from a spot of rising ground had tried in vain with telescopes to discern symptoms of its truth; when suddenly about 4 o'clock P.M. we were surprised by a loud firing of artillery, which sounded as if it were approaching nearer and nearer. The Governor-General was instantly on his horse and galloped into the field. We were all there in almost as short a time, as it takes me now to record the fact; as Sir Walter Scott would say. Unless I had been positively ordered to do so, I know not how I could have remained behind in camp along with the wonderfully apathetic bearers and khidmutgárs ([1]) *et hoc genere omni;* indeed, I was carried out of it by a sort of irresistible instinct, and my little horse was as fresh as a lark, notwithstanding the long march he had come in the morning. I could not discover, which way the Governor-General and staff had gone, and found myself among the party of the Commander-in-Chief, who just at that time came galloping up from his tent. One officer asked me whether I was prepared for the battle, and another offered me a sword, which I declined, being just as likely to cut off my own head, as any one else's. I went in search of the Governor-General's party. By this time our forces were all out in battle-array, and I had a good view of our artillery unlimbering and opening fire, and also of the flashes from the enemy's guns among the trees and bushes: a tree jungul, about three or four miles from our camp, being the awkward ground

([1]) Domestic servants.

they had taken up for their position. Several of the enemy's balls dropped near me, and my horse's legs had a narrow escape. The artillery-firing soon ceased; and I thought I should see no more of the battle. I felt disappointed: for I wanted to be in some position, whence I could command a view of the whole and watch the progress of the battle, and whence I could observe the manœuvres of the field and the principles of military science in practice, just as one observes the movements of two chess-players. This was impossible from the flatness of the ground, and also from the dust. I could only picture to myself the close combat of πικρὸς λυτὴρ νεικέων θηκτὸς σίδαρος—ὠμόφρων σίδαρος, and how δορυτίνακτος αἰθὴρ ἐπιμαίνεται. I spoke to some of the 3rd Dragoons, who had just come out of the fray, and they said that the enemy were running away towards the river, and that their cavalry, though some of them fought bravely, could only fight by dismounting from their horses, and lifting their swords with both hands at once. I soon fell in with the Governor-General and suite

BATTLE OF MOODKEE. 21

It was now growing dusk, and the enemy appeared to be retreating, though they had not given in and the conflict still raged, as it retired. Here I soon found myself in an unexpected position, and one, that none but a soldier could desire. " Every battle of the warrior is with confused noise and garments rolled in blood." Underneath our feet, as we rode along, were scattered the bodies of men, horses and camels, some gasping and others dead, while the wounded were groaning piteously and calling out for help, which we could not give; above and about our heads were whizzing bullets and cannon-balls in all directions, creating in me, I must say, a very unusual sensation. Mr. Currie remonstrated with the Governor-General for thus exposing himself to danger and importunately begged him to leave the field; but Sir Henry seemed to think differently and gave no heed to the advice. I suppose it was imprudent in the Governor-General, considering his station, and the importance of his life at such a crisis as this; and I should be inclined to say, that even in a

Commander-in-Chief such self-exposure was a thing to be avoided for the reason, which Alexander's advisers used to urge:—"οὐ γὰρ στρατηγοῦ ταῦτα, ἀλλὰ στρατιώτου εἶναι." At the same time, from what I observed, it struck me that Sir Henry's presence was of great advantage in preserving the confidence and directing the movement of a part of our force. What astonished me most was the confusion, which prevailed. But the dust and the lateness of the hour prevented one from seeing very far. The battle lasted till nearly dusk, and the enemy were driven back as far as Lohám, a village about 3 miles from Moodkee. It was quite dark before I reached my tent; and in returning home I was warned to keep at as great a distance, as I could, from the trees, lest I should be *potted at* by some evil-designing lingerer on the field. This must have been the way in which Captain Munro was shot: for the wound, just the size of a bullet, is on the top of his shoulder, and the bullet has entered in a vertical direction and most probably lodged in his spine, as he has no sensation below the middle of his back. I have been attending upon him in his tent and had no dinner. This has been a long and eventful day. It is horrible work and makes one long for the time, when wars shall cease, &c. Glory to God, that the battle is over and the victory ours! Perhaps it will be an opening for the introduction of the Gospel into another country, and thus the Prince of peace will be magnified.

19th.—I have no wish to see another battle, though I do not regret having seen this; once is enough. I have not been to visit the field to-day; but those, who have, say it is a horrid spectacle. The Seekhs have been very quick in carrying off their dead; and we are doing all we can to give to ours decent burial. Many brave men have fallen, and many a soul has departed unprepared for the world to come. I believe that the mortality on our side might have been much less; so at least they, who are the best judges, seem to think. I hear that our Sipáhees, or some of them, had the fault of firing too high, so as to miss their enemies and shoot over their heads; but there seems to be no question, that they did not *always* give too great an elevation to their muskets yesterday, and that they made the dreadful mistake of killing some of our brave Europeans—unconsciously no doubt: such was the confusion! Another instance of which confusion I must here record, viz. that one line of Sipáhees was just on the point of firing in the face of the Governor-General and of us, who were with him, when Colonel Benson rode forward and stopped them: there was nothing else to fire at. The Governor-General is as cool on the field, as I am now, while writing this. During the battle the Seekhs were beating a sort of drum or tom-tom (*k*)—to keep their courage up, I suppose, as clowns whistle in a dark night and women sing when grinding at a

(*k*) This use of the drum is very ancient and said to have been originally commemorative of an institution of Bacchus, when he visited India. Arrian says, Καὶ θεοὺς σέβειν ὅτι ἐδίδαξε Διόνυσος ἄλλους τε καὶ μάλιστα δὴ ἑωυτὸν κυμβαλίζοντας καὶ τυμπανίζοντας—ὥστε καὶ εἰς Ἀλέξανδρον ἔτι ὑπὸ κυμβάλων τε καὶ τυμπάνων ἰς τὰς μάχας Ἰνδοὺς καθίστασθαι. Hist. Ind. vii. I heard no *cymbals* at Moodkee.

mill. All however confess, that they fought very bravely. Their number is supposed to have been about 50,000.(¹) We are in possession of seventeen of their guns, and others are said to be hid in wells. Our troops have been kept under arms all day in consequence of a report, that the Seekhs were coming back upon us. It is hard work for the poor fellows; but the victory has cheered their spirits and the excitement keeps them up. Several of the Europeans have told me, that yesterday they were quite foot-sore from marching, but that, from the moment they entered the field, they felt no more of it. I think that what they accomplished yesterday is perfectly wonderful, when we contrast the exhausted state they were in from fatigue and fasting and also their paucity (a mere handful) with the freshness and superior force of the enemy. Captain Hardinge, Sir Henry's youngest son, had a narrow escape in the battle: he found himself, I hear, on the wrong side of the field.

(¹) The correct numbers are now well known, but the above was the supposition at the time.

20th.—Yesterday and to-day I have been burying the slain, *i. e.* as many as I have been requested to bury. Major Herries, Aide-de-Camp to the Governor-General, has been buried in his tent, and the Governor-General attended his funeral. (*m*) Other officers are buried under trees in the most retired spots we could select near the camp. Many, if not most, of the men have been buried on the field by their comrades, and some left unburied, the prey of dogs and vultures. The sick and wounded are quartered inside the fort of the village in tents, and a few in places like stalls for oxen. It is a melancholy scene of suffering—broken legs and broken arms, wounds in all parts of the body, groans of agony, cadaverous countenances, and so great a dearth of medical attendance, that many

(*m*) An elegant mural tablet has since been erected in the church at Barrackpore, where the Governor-General often resides, to the memory of Major Herries, of Captain Munro, another Aide-de-Camp to Sir H. Hardinge, who died from a wound received in the battle of Moodkee, and of Major Somerset, also an Aide-de-Camp, who was mortally wounded at Ferozeshahr.

of the poor men declare, that up to this time no surgeon has once visited them.

Mr. Currie came to my tent to tell me, that the Seekhs have not yet given in, that they have taken up a position about eighteen miles off, and that our army is to go out to-morrow to attack them. He expressed his regret at my being exposed to such personal danger, a contingency not foreseen when I joined the camp. We both felt that our own lives are in imminent jeopardy, and we both agreed that, if our army be beaten, it will be a just national chastisement, and that altogether it is an awful crisis calling for most earnest prayer. My hopes, however, are very buoyant.

Captain Biddulph has returned, having been set at liberty by the barbarians as soon as they heard of our victory here, and has told us all about their camp, where they carried him to, and how they kept him bound with a chain, &c. He has also given us some idea of the number of their guns, and the order in which they are disposed.

He is clothed in a long red garment, which the Seekhs put on him for decency's sake, when they dismissed him, his own dress having been taken away.

I dined with the Governor-General this evening, and after dinner he informed me, that he leaves with the troops to-morrow morning, but that I am not to go. I shall remain here and attend to the sick and wounded. May God speed them and prosper their arms!

§ 4. THE CAMP AT MOODKEE.

[I must here supply an omission in my Journal and insert between brackets a short account of my residence at Moodkee (*imprisonment* would be a more appropriate term) during the 21st, 22nd and part of the 23rd. I could write nothing in my Journal there, as orders were given for everything to be packed up and all the baggage to be collected in one place. Early in the morning of the 21st all the tents were struck, except four or five of the smallest, which afforded accommodation for us, who remained, among whom were Mr. Currie and Colonel Stuart, Secretary to Government, Military Department. All the camels and hackeries and baggage were drawn up in as close a compass as possible under the walls of the village. A native regiment and three guns were left with us, of which we should of course have made the best use, had the Seekhs paid us a visit. The guns would not have run away, though we were not quite so sure of the *pultun*.(ⁿ) I was much amused at the terror-stricken visages of my own servants the very first morning: it struck me that their fidelity would not appear to great advantage, should a body of Seekh horsemen come down to see what we were doing. Every minute of our time was lengthened by anxiety; but we expected to hear of some decisive result in the course of the first day. I remember that I felt very sanguine and confident myself. My time was chiefly occupied in going among the wounded, though it was a most unsatisfactory occupation: religious conversation did not seem to be what they wanted, either officers or men; my visits did not appear to be very welcome; and out of so many there was only one, that expressed any desire for the benefit of my services.(º) This

(ⁿ) Native regiment, a corruption of the word, "battalion."

(º) Captain Dashwood, of the Artillery, who died there from mortification caused by a wound in the leg. I saw was exceedingly painful, though not at all surprising to me, who had seen a good deal of soldiers in hospital, when I was stationed at Cánpoor; and, with regard to officers, I had never had any reason to suppose that the generality of them were at all more spiritually-minded than the mass of the common soldiers. There were also a few burials to employ part of my time. What we did for meals I almost forget; but I think it was something like a *pic-nic* the first day; the second day we were more comfortable. We heard no firing till the evening of the 21st; we heard it very distinctly during the night and the following morning. It was impossible to attempt anything like Divine Service on the 21st (Sunday): the only service, that could have been offered, must of course have been *extempore;* but, situated as I was, my mind rather revolted from the suggestion of our kneeling down together: for at the time,

him several times. I was not acquainted with him before; but I was pleased with what I saw of him, and before he died, he grasped my hand with significant earnestness.

when I might otherwise have made such a proposal, circumstances were most unfavorable to it: I was in company with a party, only one of whom appeared likely to feel an interest or to take part in such an act of worship. Several deserters from our native army came in during the action. A British Officer was sent in with a message; and he gave us to understand, that, when he left the field, it was impossible to know which way things would turn. At last on the morning of the 23rd, we were relieved from our suspense by the arrival of a messenger with a note from Colonel Benson written in pencil and announcing, to our indescribable joy, that a glorious and decisive victory had been gained over the enemy, and that the camp might proceed to Ferozepoor without delay. We were not long in bidding adieu to Moodkee.]

§ 5. THE BATTLE OF FEROZESHAHR.

*25th.—Ferozepoor.—*I arrived here on the 23rd from Moodkee in company with Mr. Currie and a few others, who had stayed with the camp. We came not over the field of Ferozeshahr, but by a more direct road, a distance of about eighteen miles, and rode as fast as we could, eager to hear the particulars of another victory, the glad tidings of which had summoned us away from Moodkee, that never-to-be-forgotten place of suspense and anxiety. On our road we passed several dead bodies and other remains of the first action, and put to flight numbers of vagabond plunderers (*p*). and saw a mine explode not far from us, and heard the report of several others. I am now in my tent again, and our camp is pitched in its usual style.

(*p*) These are wretches, who after battle prowl about the field to see what they can pick up.

On first arriving, I was obliged to go with Mr. Currie to General Littler's house, where the Governor-General was staying, there being no chaplain here, nor any acquaintance at whose house I could put up. I dined that evening with the Governor-General; it was a cold dinner, but I dare say Sir Henry never enjoyed one more; and we were all in *dishabille*, but that agreed better with the disorder of the rooms, and the *tout ensemble* of confusion. All faces had gathered brightness; though the gladness that prevailed was of a temperate, sober, dignified character—a moderation in the joy of triumph resulting, it is to be hoped, from the influence of the Christian religion. How different this from the unbridled exultation and riotous mirth of heathens! The Governor-General's countenance wore a happy and collected smile; but he talked with great excitement of the crisis, which was just over, and there was the manifest ebb of the agitation of one, that had seen the danger and foreseen the consequences of our defeat.

The action was fought on the 21st and 22nd at a place called Ferozeshahr about eight miles off, where the enemy had taken up a very strong and formidable position, and it was a *dubium certamen* for a long while. More than once great fears were entertained; and I hear that the presence and personal courage of the Governor-General at a critical moment of the battle were of the greatest value. He had offered his services to the Commander-in-Chief as second in command, and they had been gladly accepted. Our danger was in great measure owing to the extreme exhaustion of our troops, who had no provisions with them, and were therefore half-perishing with fatigue from the long march together with hunger and thirst, and were either lying on the bare cold ground, or else fighting through the night of the 21st. This 21st, though Sunday, was no sabbath to them: inexorable necessity made it as hard a work-day, as ever wrung the sweat from the human brow; still it was the Lord's day, and, if the Lord's work was done in it, as I believe it was, the truest Christian breathing has it not within his power to charge our arms with guilt for their operations on that day. The cold in the morning of the 22nd was so bitter, that the men could hardly handle their muskets, and the thirst so intense during the day, that they were driven to drink putrid water, which at another time would have been rejected as poison, and the horses were almost mad. The Governor-General had his share of the common sufferings and privations. The end of all was a decisive victory with the capture of the enemy's guns.

Had we been beaten, the consequences for a time at least would in all probability have been dreadful: one shudders at the imagination of them. There was nothing on our part to prevent the barbarians, infuriated with triumph, from marching down the country and committing, as they went, every species of violence and outrage. We, who were in durance at Moodkee, should have fallen among their earliest victims. They would not have gone so far as London, the point they had proposed to themselves for the terminus of their career, but they would have gone quite far enough to give a terrible blow to the *préstige* of the British name in Asia, if not in Europe. Who can tell what a shock might have been communicated to the equilibrium of powers in Europe? As for America, the war-party there would have been louder than ever; and most likely desperate conflicts with the British would have been raging in both hemispheres at once. Thank God, however, that disastrous extremity has been averted; and here we are still in the proud position of conquerors underneath the refuge of His everlasting arms. Truly, "there is none like unto the God of Jeshurun." And surely the hand of the Deity stretched forth to defend us was as visible on this occasion, as was the danger, which called for His protection. Evidently the Governor-General is disposed to acknowledge this. He expressed a wish, that I should allude to-day to the late victories and to the righteousness of our cause, and that the glory should be ascribed to God. I discoursed upon Luke ii. 14. The attendance was surprisingly small — shamefully small.(*q*) Perhaps many of those, who were absent, think that such Service is *humbug*, or waste of time, or that our cause is not good, or that the Almighty has nothing to do with such affairs, that it is all *luck*, &c. What will they think in the day of judgment? What reason will they then render for their absence from this Service? The ingratitude and ungodliness of the Christian world not only will justify the wrath of an insulted God hereafter, but magnifies His mercy and forbearance now. With what truth may we exclaim, " Not unto us, O Lord, not unto us, &c.—for our iniquities justly call for vengeance upon us!" His long-suffering is inexplicable on the supposition of no hell in the world to come. I read the thanksgiving appointed in the Prayer-Book for such occasions, " O Almighty God, who

(*q*) The public are well aware that the Governor-General had *invited every British subject* at Ferozepoor to come to his tent and join him in this service of prayer and thanksgiving. See notification by Governor-General, dated Ferozepoor, 26th December, 1845.

art a strong tower, &c." I felt that it was too short and too general, and regretted that I was not at liberty to use any other besides.

The night of the 23rd I slept on a sofa in a *bungla*(^r) belonging to an Officer of the Station, having been taken there by a member of our camp, who knew him. It was deserted and nearly empty, as all the houses were: the inhabitants having left them in a panic and gone for refuge into the fort. The natives also had all run away from the bazaars and hidden themselves somewhere; though it seems a mystery, where they could have gone and remained for so many days together, as it is an open desert all round. Yesterday morning I came into camp.

This is without exception the most dusty place I ever saw in my life. Roads there are none, there being no foundation for them. To step outside one's tent is to be smothered with dust.

(^r) *Bungla*, a thatched house, built entirely on the ground-floor, the usual kind of residence of Europeans in India.

The bottom of the graves in the burial-ground is as fine and impalpable dust as the top, however deep they may be dug; and they fall in almost as fast as they are made: it is quite dangerous to stand near them. In the dusk of the evening it is as difficult to find one's way, as in a London fog. It is nothing but dust wherever one goes; and the whole country round seems a desert of dust. It is not sandy dust, which would be heavier, but pulverized alluvial soil: so that the poet unconsciously gave a literal description of Ferozepoor dust, when he wrote

.... κάσις
πηλοῦ ξύνουρος διψία κόνις............

No doors or windows will keep it out; and they say that it penetrates into the works of watches.

§ 6. CAMP AT FEROZEPOOR.

26th.—I have constant calls to the burial-ground, which is a long way off. The Governor-General attended at the funeral of Major Broadfoot, for whom he felt the greatest esteem. Many corpses lie on the field unburied, "meat for the fowls of the heaven and for the beasts of the earth." " Cœlo tegitur, qui non habet urnam." Those, who have been to visit the field since the battle, describe it as a horrid spectacle. I have always been struck with the great importance, which soldiers attach to the rite of burial—an importance almost superstitious. It is the more remarkable on account of the less importance which they generally attach to other ordinances and to the essential parts of religion; and also because heathen soldiers, from whom the majority of so-called Christian soldiers differ so little, used to pride themselves upon looking forward with magnanimity to the abandonment and exposure of their bodies after death. Decent burial ought of course to be given, where it can; and a service for the grave like that in our Prayer-Book is very full of comfort, and is calculated also to impart sublimity to the thoughts of mourners; but I must confess I think that burial ought to be to Christians the least important of all religious rites; and I fear that very often there is more superstition associated with the ceremony, than is becoming in heirs of immortality. I for my part would rather sympathize on an occasion like this with the widow and the orphan; and though I deny not that the want of sepulture may be a thing to be lamented, I would rather grieve in reflecting, how few of those corpses yonder have been temples of the Holy Ghost. How many have been cut off in the midst of their days with the pollution of their sins upon them!

28*th.*—(Sunday.)—Divine Service was held in the Governor-General's tent. The congregation small. To-day at dinner the Governor-General requested me to say grace every day: a request, with which I fear it will be difficult always to comply: for the band strikes up the moment we take our places at the table. I often wonder why this custom of "saying grace" is so generally confined to dinner: why should it be observed at one meal and not at another? This evening we heard that the Seekhs have entirely abandoned this side of the river. They are not, however, finally subdued, and will, no doubt, fight desperately with us as soon as we cross over to the other side, and will hold out as long as they have any artillery left. They have already held out longer than we anticipated; and it is not likely that they will give in, till they are completely crushed: they are brave men and moreover have nothing now, but the success of their arms, to trust to: they are fighting for *rotee pánee*. (*) The struggle once over, if it should terminate in our favour, there can be little

(*) Bread and water.

doubt that we shall be a blessing to their country. The prospect of this may reconcile us to the bloodshed. The Government of Lahore, if the name *Government* be not misapplied, would be glad to come to terms with us now; but they are afraid of their own revolutionary army and are anxiously waiting for us to destroy it. They have been exhibiting a singular example of oriental duplicity, and cunningly preparing for either result, the triumph of the Khalsa or that of the British arms, which latter they now perhaps expect as the more probable of the two. This evening I went to the hospitals, the barracks being converted into hospitals for the occasion, where about 900 wounded and sick Europeans are lying. I wish to let them all know that there is a Protestant Minister at hand. I should be very glad indeed, if the Christian duty urged by the Apostle James (ch. v. *v.* 14) were more attended to, than it is: I mean the duty of *calling for* the Elder of the Church. This duty often seems to be quite forgotten; while a Minister is always accused of negligence, if he do not visit the sick, though he be not called for and frequently, perhaps generally, not wanted. If a Clergyman were really wanted, there can be little doubt that he would be applied to with as much eagerness and importunity, as a Counsellor or Physician is. The visits of Jesus were solicited for bodily cures. We hear a great deal said about the duty and advantage of Chaplains " administering the consolations of religion" to soldiers in hospital. This sounds very fine and sentimental; but what does it mean? It is well known that soldiers, with very few exceptions, are the last subjects in the world for these said *consolations*. Men, who are hardened in iniquity, whose " neck is an iron sinew and their brow brass," are not the men to understand or to want such *consolations:* they have need rather to be persuaded by " the terrors of the Lord" to flee from the wrath to come. I have only been "called for" once at all since the wounds and sickness began. (¹) Captain Dashwood, who died in the

(¹) Of course, the Governor-General's camp, to which I

fort at Moodkee from mortification of the leg, sent and asked me to administer the Lord's supper to him. He died in the evening of the same day;

was attached, was the proper sphere of my duty; but, as there was no Chaplain appointed for the Army, it was soon generally known that my services were available for all. I am aware that the passage above quoted, James v. 14, 15, refers, or is understood to refer, to the cure of bodily sickness; but it also refers to absolution and forgiveness of sin. Besides, if anxiety for spiritual benefits were as great as for temporal, would not this passage be eagerly appealed to by the Laity themselves as justifying their solicitation of the counsel and prayers of the Clergy?

In accordance with Scripture, "the Order for the Visitation of the Sick" directs thus:—"When any person is sick, notice shall be given thereof to the Minister of the Parish." For want of this notice, I have frequently been ignorant of the existence of cases of illness in Stations and Districts, where I have been Chaplain, till I have afterwards discovered it in the abuse and invective heaped upon me for inattention to them. We visit the sick with readiness and pleasure—at least those within the sphere of our duty and within the limits of our time and ability; but this readiness can only be supposed on condition of "notice being given," and the pleasure is enhanced an hundred fold, when we know that our services are wanted and our authority recognised.

With regard to soldiers in hospital it is true, that the

and it was a delightful satisfaction to me, judging by outward appearance, to think that he departed in peace with God. Four officers belonging to the Governor-General's camp have been wounded severely, and two of them have died of their wounds; yet neither of these latter has of himself desired to see me for any spiritual purpose. One of them, of whom I had formed a favourable impression from the little I knew of him, died with his Prayer-Book by his side; and we buried it along with him: but he never asked nor sent for me, nor, when I visited him, did he express a wish himself to talk about his soul. I hope the end of this man was peace, though I have a mixed feeling about him; I hope he is now in Abraham's bosom and hereafter will be found in the blessed regions of immortality.

29*th.*—People talk of monuments to the dead—regular visits of a Chaplain, where one is appointed, are an understood arrangement, which implies that vicarious notice has been given. But, notwithstanding, this we should like to hear individual wishes and solicitations more frequently expressed by the soldiers themselves.

I hear it said that the brave men, who have fallen, ought to be immortalized by some monument to their memory. Well, but Christians know of a better immortality; besides ἀνδρῶν ἐπιφανῶν πᾶσα γῆ τάφος; there is no want of a monument in any particular locality to preserve the brave deeds of our countrymen from falling into oblivion, or to testify our commendation of them: they will live and be honoured in the memories of all men and in the record of history. Pericles himself had almost said that στῆλαι might be dispensed with. (*u*)

Numbers of our Sipáhees are said to have been in Ferozepoor on the night of the 21st instead of in the field. But, still more strange and disgusting, more than one *British Officer*, I hear, turned heart-sick and deserted his post. It would really be difficult to credit this, were it not that the evidence of its truth is too clear; but this being the case, one must believe it, however loath to do

(*u*) He did not *quite* say so (see Thucyd. ii. 42), but then he and his countrymen were heathens.

so. I look upon such men with the utmost contempt and think they deserve to be blown away from the cannon's mouth — ignominious cowards, who desert their country in the hour of danger—I say that each one of them is a despicable traitor,

> "Unworthy of the blessings of the brave,
> Is base in kind and born to be a slave."

One does not feel so much surprise and indignation at the fidelity of Sipáhees giving way sometimes: mercenaries are mercenaries all the world over. But for a man to call himself a Briton and turn coward in the field is perfectly horrible, and can only be compared to the treachery of a man, who calls himself a Christian and betrays his Lord in the hour of temptation.

The Governor-General is evidently anxious. He sees before him an enemy still active and formidable, and he is also aware that the affections of the natives, subjects of the British Government, in this part of the country are not so well disposed towards us, as could be wished. Were any reverse to befall us, they would instantly turn against us. The Governor-General is very kind in directing every attention to be paid to the wounded Sipáhees, though, poor creatures, they seem to be very much neglected, and many have died for want of medical attendance or of food (*).

Jan. 4th, 1846.—(Sunday.)—Divine Service in the Governor-General's tent. Some of the people of the Station attended. This Station is badly off at present, having neither Church nor Chaplain; though I believe a Chaplain has been appointed. The want of the means of public worship and other privileges connected with the presence of a Clergyman is much complained of; and truly it is a great evil and a very manifest one: where there is nothing external to remind them of it, how soon do the majority of professing Christians forget

(*) I ought to have added that his attention to the British soldiers in hospital was as considerate and kind as possible. He used to visit the hospitals himself, and so did Sir Hugh Gough; and the Governor-General sent them their Christmas fare from his own kitchen.

religion altogether and particularly the observance of the Lord's day!

Yesterday two soldiers came to me, to know whether I could marry them without a License and without the usual delay of publication of Banns, as they could not tell how soon they might be ordered to march; I told them that compliance with their request would be contrary to the Law of Marriage. It is a distressing case to all parties. Might not the Law of Marriage contain some provision for such cases, as this? They no doubt are frequently occurring; and, though the law is definite and clear for his guidance, a Clergyman may very often be placed in a painful and perplexing situation. The women, whom the soldiers wish to marry, are widows—their husbands having been slain, or having died of their wounds, last month; and, if they are not married again within six months or obtain some other means of support, they lose their allowance and become destitute.

7th.—I visit the hospitals daily. It is as much

as I can do, to go through two or three hospitals a-day. Why is no Chaplain here, and why is not another appointed with the army, whose proper work it would be to attend to the hospitals and whom I might assist? Indeed six Chaplains would not be too many for this sphere of labour at the present time. (*) I grieve to find that there is very little demand or desire for my services; nor do I discover much difference between men suffering in this way from wounds and men suffering from ordinary sickness: there is the

(*) I may here remark, that a great deal was afterwards said in the Newspapers about the activity of some Priest or Priests of the Church of Rome in attending the hospital, but that I never once fell in with any such Minister during the whole time, either at the hospitals or at the burial-ground, or anywhere else, and that I never heard him once spoken of. Still it does not follow that no such Priest was present; and my remark is not made from any wish to disparage the zeal and activity of the Church of Rome, in which respects, as well as in others, she generally sets us a bright example. A Priest of that Church was killed, I believe, in the battle of Moodkee; but *we* do not consider a field of battle the appropriate place for *our* ministerial services.

same general recklessness and hardness of heart, the same offence at the name of Christ. Still there are a few exceptions, and these few afford one great consolation. One or two of the men have told me that they had their Bibles in their knapsacks with them on the field of battle, and that they did not find it impossible to think of God and to pray to Him even in that hour of excitement and confusion. The gross ignorance of many is perfectly astounding. One day I asked a man, why he was called a Christian, what the word Christian meant, and who the Mediator was; he said that he did not know. This wretch had a Prayer-book at the very time under his pillow, and no doubt had been accustomed to the same opportunities of instruction, as others, in " all things, which a Christian ought to know and believe to his soul's health." This is only one out of many such instances of wilful ignorance, hardness of heart, and contempt of God's Word, which I meet with and which vividly remind me of my hospital-experience at Cánpoor.

11th. — (Sunday.) — Divine Service in the Governor-General's tent. A fair congregation.

16th.—Diarrhœa is prevalent just now in our camp. It is not known exactly, to what cause its prevalence is to be assigned. Some attribute it to the air, others to the water; the dust escapes imputation. But what can there be in the air at this season of the year? and as for the water, all drink it alike, though all are not affected by this disorder, and it has the reputation among the residents here of being remarkably pure and good and materially conducive to their health. The cause remains an enigma. Horses are suffering from the same complaint. Ferozepoor has the name of being a very healthy place all the year round in spite of its uninviting appearance. I should suppose this very likely: the dryness of the soil and the openness of the country must contribute much to its salubrity. But certainly the selection of such a spot by Hygieia says little in favour of her taste for the picturesque.

21st.—Last night I had an interesting discussion

with one of our party, originating with the question, what benefits we, as a nation, have conferred upon India. It is astonishing what opposite opinions men form upon this, as upon almost every subject. He maintained that the British have imparted no civilization nor any good whatever to the people of this country. As for the Christian religion, he did not believe that there was a single convert to Christianity in the whole of India. He denied that Providence has appointed us to come into this and other lands, or that we are His instruments for benefiting and converting the heathen, or that "Providence troubles itself at all about such matters." He considered that we have no more right to the title of God's chosen people, than the Mohummedans have; and he did not see why the Kurán might not be the Word of God. He was not aware of anything remarkable in the present state of the Jews, and did not understand why it should be called a standing miracle. He thought there was no doctrinal difference between the Protestant and the Papist; and that there was no more idolatry in the Church of Rome, than in that of England. He regarded the Church of Rome as a militant Church, ours as a dominant, and looked upon the Priests of the former as more resembling the Apostolic character, than the Clergy of the latter; and he spoke with the utmost contempt of the haughtiness of our Bishops, rolling about in costly carriages and leaving large legacies to their children, in contrast with the lowliness of Jesus Christ, who went about bare-footed and had not where to lay His head. Such were the opinions of my opponent; and with the exception of the last, referring to Bishops, for which there is too much foundation, I will add, such are the wretched infidel opinions, which abound and are rampant in the Christian world. These men, I am persuaded, are not so few, as is sometimes imagined; and they are very active enemies of the cross of Christ; they disseminate their pernicious principles and do the work of the Devil, their employer, with great success; " the poison of asps is under their lips;" and they forcibly remind one of that "old serpent," who beguiled Eve through his subtlety. So much the more need for our watchfulness and readiness at all times and in all places "to convince gainsayers" and "endure contradiction."

This evening at the hospital of H. M. 80th, a hardened wretch of the name of Ore told me, that he was a stranger to my principles and did not wish me to converse with him. He said he had been brought up in unbelief and felt no uneasiness of mind at the prospect of dying an unbeliever. He called himself a worm. On my reminding him that he had a soul, which was precious, as well as a vile body, he said that a man need not be under any alarm with respect to futurity, if he did his duty towards his fellow-creatures. He could not condemn himself of having done otherwise. If he was corrupt, God had made him so. It was *unreasonable* to suppose that God would punish him for being what He made him. He did not believe in an evil spirit. He had read the Bible, but did not believe it to be the Word of God. He had understood that the writings of the Apostles were forgeries, composed after their death. He spoke of the differences and animosity among Ministers of the Christian religion as an argument against its truth. He could not believe that any men were ever so superior to others, as to be inspired of God. He could not exactly disprove the truth of the Bible, but still he could not see why he should not regard it as false. He did not condemn it: on the contrary, he approved of the morality it inculcates. He did not deny that it might be true, but he could not see why he should trouble himself about it or be at all anxious to inquire upon the subject. He felt quite satisfied as he was. When I mentioned the atonement made for human guilt, he said nothing in reply. He gave me credit for good motives and intentions in talking with him, but he would rather keep to his own principles. So I left this stout-hearted son of Belial to the enjoyment of his cogitations and his prospects of the world to come. Such cases, I know alas! too well, are not uncommon

CAMP AT FEROZEPOOR.   59

among soldiers. I have witnessed many such in the course of my hospital-experience in this country; but never, I think, one that shocked me more than this. I felt as if I were talking with the Devil himself face to face.

22nd.—I had the satisfaction to-day of administering the Sacrament of the Lord's Supper to four officers together, one of whom is in a dying state from flesh-wounds: poor fellow! he is almost hacked to pieces, and it is astonishing that he has survived so long. (*)

25th.—(Sunday.)—Divine Service was held, as usual, in the Governor-General's tent. There has been a great outcry here against the negligence of the Authorities in not having provided a Church and Chaplain for this station. Why then do not the residents avail themselves of the present opportunity of attending public worship more freely

(*) His name was Egerton. One of the other communicants was the late Col. Codrington, whose soul, we hope, now rests in peace. I had visited Col. Codrington before in the rude hospital at Moodkee.

than they do? They all know, or might know, if they would, that they are at perfect liberty to come here every Sunday. Very few of them, however, attend. I should like to see a better proof of their sincerity.

27th.—To-day I received from a friend two parcels of tracts of the Society for Promoting Christian Knowledge, for the men in the hospitals. (*) It was his own spontaneous thought; and nothing could have been more acceptable at the present crisis. We are at a great loss for books. The regimental library of H. M. 61st, like most libraries of this kind, contains but a scanty sprinkling of religious books. Every soldier of course is understood to have his Bible, *i. e.*, in peaceful times; but Bibles are exceedingly scarce in such times as these. The tracts certainly will not go very far among so many: still they are a help, and I trust they may do some good, and so multiply themselves, as it were, like

(*) The friend was the late lamented Mr. Norgate, then Chaplain at Agra.

the loaves and fishes. Many a man too, I believe, will read a tract, that would not have courage to read his Bible in the sight of his comrades.

29th.—This morning we were all cheered by the glad tidings of another victory gained over the enemy at Alliwál by the division under Sir H. Smith, a junction having been formed with the Loodiána force. There was a muttering the other day about some reverse, that our arms had sustained in that quarter.(*) I know nothing of the particulars; but, whatever the reverse may have been, I suppose that it will now be swallowed up by the success which has followed it. The enemy crossed over to this side of the river with about fifty guns and 20,000 men. (*a*) The engagement

(*) The skirmish on the 21st, at Buddiwál, is now as well known, as the battle at Alliwál on the 28th. The best generals are liable to commit blunders sometimes. Alexander himself in crossing the Hydaspes, previously to his engagement with Porus, made a mistake, for the like to which what storms of invective would public opinion have poured upon the head of a Lord Gough in the present day!

(*a*) The correct numbers are now known.

was fought yesterday. They were completely beaten and driven back to the other side of the river, and all their guns captured. Hundreds of them were drowned in re-crossing. To the God of battles be ascribed the glory; though miserable is the havoc, which glorifies Him.

This victory is considered very opportune: as some event of the kind was wanted to raise the spirits of our army and to keep up the impression created throughout the country by the intelligence of Moodkee and Ferozeshahr, so long a period of inaction having followed upon those victories without any symptoms of the termination of the war.

The men in hospital are wonderfully refreshed by the good news.

February 1st.—(Sunday.)—Divine Service as usual. A full congregation. I discoursed on the 3rd Commandment. It is quite awful to hear how the name of God is taken in vain by young officers and other members of the Camp in their ordinary daily conversation with each other: scarcely a sentence is uttered without it.

CAMP AT FEROZEPOOR.

2nd.—I hear that my sermon yesterday caused great offence. God be praised for the force of truth. It is remarkable that even in this desert and at this dry time of the year there are patches of vegetation, which somewhat relieve the eye; but chiefly in the direction of the river. Nearer to the river we are not surprised to find large crops and whole fields of refreshing green. The way in which these patches of vegetation are produced, where there is not a natural hollow in the ground, is said to be the artificial formation of gentle hollows in the flat surface of the soil, so that in the rainy season the water may lodge in them and a fertilizing moisture remain throughout the year. There are also in some places wells worked with the Persian wheel for the purpose of irrigation. Some of the houses in the station have gardens attached to them, in which European vegetables vie with marigolds; the cauliflower is remarkably fine.

Thermometer at noon inside tent 62° Fahrh.

5th.—Thermometer at noon inside tent 72° Fahrh.

8*th.*—(Sunday.)—Divine Service as usual. Full congregation.

9*th.*—The Governor-General went out to-day to the Commander-in-Chief's Camp, about twenty miles off. The infidel above mentioned of the name of Ore expired on the 3rd. I hear that just before his death he said to one of his comrades, " I have seen my folly." I cannot find out however what he meant; and the expression by itself is very ambiguous. Though he had many relations in England, he left his property to the orphan child of one of his comrades.

Another glorious victory was gained over the Seekhs this morning at Sobráon on the river-side about twenty miles from here. The battle appears to have lasted about four hours. We heard the firing very distinctly. So much for the formidable entrenchments of Sobráon, which have been looking defiance at us for a long and wearisome time. Many thought the position of the enemy with their tremendous τειχῆ γήϊνα next to impregnable. There is an end of them now, however, as

BATTLE OF SOBRAON.   65

well as of most of those, who built them. All their guns are captured, themselves discomfited with a terrible slaughter, and thousands drowned in recrossing the river—reminding us of the Egyptian host and the Red Sea. Justice has been dealt them by Him, who has fought for us, and we thank Him for it and so will the whole country, which has been released from the fury of its oppressors. (*b*) " Thy right hand, O Lord, is

(*b*) I see nothing unchristian, as some do, in rejoicing at the destruction of wickedness and in thanking God for it. We are taught by Scripture to do so—by the same Scripture, which teaches us to be merciful and tender-hearted. It is a mistake moreover, in my opinion, to suppose that in such a feeling there is anything more suited to the temper of the Jewish dispensation, than to that of the Christian. God's word is one and the same throughout. Personal hatred is forbidden no less in the Old Testament, than in the New; but that is a very different thing from rejoicing at the overthrow of the enemies of our country and the deliverance of the oppressed from ungodly and savage monsters of lust and cruelty; in this I can see nothing more Jewish, than Christian. In self-defence I might kill a man and rejoice at having got rid of him, without in the least degree breaking the Divine law, " Love your enemies."

become glorious in power; thy right hand, O Lord, hath dashed in pieces the enemy. In the greatness of thine excellency thou hast overthrown them, that rose up against thee." "This is the day of the Lord God of hosts, a day of vengeance, that he may avenge him of his adversaries. The sword hath devoured and been satiate and been made drunk with their blood." "Woe to the bloody city! it is all full of lies and robbery. Behold, I am against thee, saith the Lord of hosts. There is no healing of thy bruise; thy wound is grievous; all that hear the bruit of thee shall clap their hands over thee: for upon whom hath not thy wickedness passed continually?" It is expected that the Seekhs have now had enough of the Faringees and will give in and surrender all hopes of paying a visit to London. Our swords, however, must still remain drawn: as we do not know whether or not they may be inclined to try us again. They are infatuated; that is quite clear already. And they are inflamed with fanatical frenzy, which drives them headlong. It seems to be a remarkable case of ὕβρις and Ἐριννύς, as the ancient Greeks would have said. One cannot help remembering the line—

ἀλλ' ὅταν σπεύδῃ τις αὐτὸς, χὡ θεὸς ξυνάπτεται.

11*th*.—Our army is to cross the river immediately and march straight up to Lahore; though things have been managed so skilfully, that up to this time it has not been known, except by a few necessarily in the secret, whereabouts our bridge of boats was to be constructed. Secresy has been the order of the day. No one in camp knew on the evening of the 9th, except the Governor-General and those immediately about him, that he was about to start on the following morning to the Commander-in-Chief's camp and that the attack was then to be made on the enemy. They were effectually taken by surprise. The battle is described to have been a beautiful sight, every movement of our troops to have been distinctly visible from the ground occupied by the Governor-General and Staff, and the whole to have resembled the order and steadiness of evolutions in a review. This was what I wanted to see at Moodkee; but there was nothing of the kind to be seen on that occasion, all was disorder and confusion. The Seekhs, they say, fought furiously; and there were numbers of naked Akálees among them, whose presence maddened them the more and who are represented to have looked like fiends. Several officers, who never saw a battle in their lives before this of Sobráon, declare that it exceeded all their ideas and expectations, and that the shot of all sorts, which kept pouring around them, was literally without exaggeration as thick as hail. Every man must feel more or less astonished the first time he is under fire, and scarcely know at some moments whether his head is on or off his shoulders; but the oldest soldier must acknowledge that a storm of cannon, grape and musket-shot, like this, is no joke. Sir R. Dick has fallen at Sobráon. I remember that brave general telling me, that he never went into battle without first going down upon his knees, though it might be on the bare ground, and

BATTLE OF SOBRAON. 69

offering up a prayer in Christ's name for the forgiveness of his sins. I suppose therefore he did so on this occasion. There is nothing inconsistent between praying and fighting, as some are stupid enough to think. There were soldiers, I know (few indeed, but still soldiers), whose prayers went up to heaven as well as mine from the field of Moodkee. (ᶜ)

12*th*. — The accounts of the numbers, who perished in the river, are perfectly amazing.

(ᶜ) A man needs not "*the acquired habits of the ecclesiastic*" to be able to pray on a field of battle. The ministrations of a Clergyman however in the hour of mortal combat are quite another matter, and I would refer the reader to some very sensible remarks upon this subject in a little book called " Religio militis," the author of which was evidently a military man, and which ought to be in the hands of every British soldier. In order that my meaning may not be misunderstood, I will just observe that he says, what to any one, that has been eye-witness of a battle, must be perfectly obvious, that at such an hour such ministrations would be importune and worse than useless. I need not add that the author speaks of a *Protestant* Minister. The usefulness of a Papal Priest, who has the mysterious power of charming a soul out of the jaws of Hell by a word or a touch or the clink of a rupee, is another question.

Some say 5,000, others declare they could not have been less than 8,000! I have heard the Commander-in-Chief himself say that he was sure the bodies were so thick, that he could have walked over to the other side of the river by stepping from one to the other. Their bridge, which they had made, had been blown up, and in their panic they missed the ford. In all that occurred we see the hand of an over-ruling Providence and the same protecting arm, which fought for Israel of old.

§ 7. ENTERING THE PUNJAB.

14*th.*—The Governor-General crossed the Sutlej this morning. The greater part of our army had gone before. He was accompanied by all his suite, except Mr. Edwards, Capt. Johnstone and myself, who expect to follow in a few days. The bridge is just above Khoonda Ghát, about four miles off. It is a double bridge of boats, which were made and sent up the river for this purpose a year ago, each armed with a gun—the famous pontoon bridge of Lord Ellenborough, who, it is commonly said, would have used it long before this. The policy of the present ruler has the advantage of being just, as well as successful. Not that a different policy would have been condemned as unjust by all writers on the principles of warfare: for instance, the "Counsel Learned Extraordinary" to King James I. lays down the maxim, "that a just fear, without an actual invasion or offence, is a sufficient ground

of a war and in the nature of a true defensive."
(Considerations touching a war with Spain). But
Sir H. Hardinge certainly cannot be charged with
provocation of the war: and his forbearance and
political honesty, so far as they have gone, have
been rewarded with at least as triumphant a
result, as would have been the precipitation,
which another man at the head of our government
might have thought expedient. Together with
the forbearance of a just and magnanimous ruler,
he has displayed also the utmost sagacity and
wisdom: events, as well as the previous increase
of the army, prove that he was not unprepared
for the contest. He is blamed by some for ever
having allowed the pontoon bridge to be brought
up to Ferozepoor, this being considered enough
to provoke a war. Surely this was nothing more
than a wise and necessary precaution: — the
provocation commenced with our enemies long
before. The probability is, that not one man in
a hundred would have acted more sagaciously,
than he has done, and that not one man in a

ENTERING THE PUNJAB. 73

hundred in his position, however he might have acted, would have escaped obloquy.

This river Sutlej, or Suloodr, or Suttudra, is the ancient Hysudrus of Pliny and Zaradrus of Ptolemy. (*d*) The Becas, which forms a junction with it higher up, is the ancient Hyphasis of Arrian and Upasis of Pliny. It is amusing to hear the false quantities. The Hyphasis and the Acesines are the only two of the five rivers, that can easily be mispronounced; and these are cruelly distorted by some of my military brethren, or *murdered*, as my Schoolmaster used to say. One would really think they were the Germans whom he used to speak of: "*nos Germāni quantitātem syllabārum non curāmus.*" The Sutlej is a most erratic river: I believe it changes its course more or less every year. (*e*)

(*d*) Suloodr—Zaradrus. To Oriental scholars it is well known that the interchange of *l* and *r* and of the other liquids is very common in the East; nor is the variation confined to Oriental languages.

(*e*) In the beginning of last year the river had swept away a great part of the field of Sobráon.

With regard to the war the common impression seems to be, that it is now nearly at an end, and that the Seekhs have been thoroughly beaten. It has been astonishing to observe the extreme apathy of the servile classes of natives during all this time of suspense and anxiety. Even while the battles were going on and the report of the firing was distinctly heard in camp, these wretches appeared as unconcerned as mere vegetables. *Pysa* and *khána*(¹) seemed, as usual, to absorb the whole of their attention. I do not believe that the lower orders of natives feel the slightest interest in anything of importance that occurs around them, nor that they care one straw what becomes of their country; so long as they can get enough to eat and ground to sleep on. The only excitement they are capable of in such times, as these, is the instinct to run away, should danger come near enough. What a melancholy state of

(¹) *Pysa* is a small copper coin and the general term used by the lower order of natives for their money: *khána* is food.

degradation! It is impossible also not to discern the difference between the Sipáhee and the British Soldier in respect of patriotic spirit and even *esprit de corps:* nor is this to be wondered at. The thing to be wondered at is, that any observers of the native character and sentiments should endeavour to make out that there is little or no difference. "Jack Sepoy" highly approves of security of person and property (as who does not?) and admires the system of regular pay, extra pay, batta and so forth; and so long as he derives such advantages from the British Government, he will steadfastly and bravely fight for the Queen of England. But yet he is influenced φόβῳ μᾶλλόν τι ἢ εὐνοίᾳ τῇ πρὸς ἡμᾶς, as Alexander said of his mercenaries.

15th.—(Sunday.)—I held Divine service in Mr. Edwards' tent, himself and seven or eight clerks belonging to the Foreign Office being present.

17th. — A message having arrived yesterday from the Governor-General, that all was quiet and that we were to proceed to join him, we started this morning and marched to *Kussoor*, fifteen miles from Ferozepoor, and eleven from the bridge—almost as glad to turn our backs upon Ferozepoor, as we were upon Moodkee. Kussoor, in former days a Mohummedan town, is now a place of ruins and very picturesque. I arrived just in time to catch a sight of Rájah Gooláb Singh, who had come from Lahore, for the purpose of negotiating a treaty on behalf of his Government, and was just on the point of mounting his elephant to return to his own camp. We are yet in uncertainty as to what has become of the remnant of the Seekh army. Whether they have given in, or mean to try another encounter, is unknown; only the former is presumed.

18*th.—Lulliána*, eleven miles.—The Governor-General held a durbár for the reception of Rájah Gooláb Singh and the little Máharájah Dhuleep Singh. They came upon elephants, but in plain attire and altogether with the mien of humiliation suited to their present condition. The terms we have exacted from the Government of Lahore are the payment of a million and half of money, as compensation for the expenses of the war; that the Seekh army receive no more pay, until they disband; that the Máharájah be placed upon the throne; and that the rich tract of country called the Jullunder Dooáb, lying between the Sutlej and the Beeas, the most fertile in the whole Punjáb, be ceded to the British Government.

19th.—Kutch.—The Rájah held a durbár, at which some of the Governor-General's Staff attended. They described the tents as being magnificent, lined with Cashmere shawls, &c. It is said that a bloody battle was fought in this neighbourhood by Alexander the Great. Very likely, though it is impossible to identify the names of places at this distance of time; and no doubt, were our little world to last so long, the spots of Moodkee, Ferozeshahr, Alliwál, and Sobráon, would retain their celebrity for an equal period of years, *i. e.* upwards of 2,000, a celebrity, which in all probability would outlive their names. Arrian says that Alexander took a city called

Sangala, which made a brave resistance, somewhere in this region: for it was between the Hydraotes or Rávee and the Hyphasis or Beeas. But this is all we know; the spot it is impossible to determine: perhaps it was much higher up. (*o*) What an interesting country to be traversing! How little did any of us in our school-boy days dream that we should ever be treading ground so famous in the history of the Macedonian conqueror! Another reflection too still more interesting arises—a reflection upon the difference between his *causa belli* and ours, between his motive and that of our Governor-General or the Commander-in-Chief of our forces in bringing an army to this part of the world. His was mere lust of aggressive conquest, ours in self-defence against an aggressive enemy: whence we may

(*o*) An interesting and creditable essay has been since written in the Journal of the Asiatic Society of Bengal, No. iii., 1852, on the sites of Nikaia and Boukephalon, by Major James Abbott, in which he endeavours to trace Alexandrian marches and engagements in the Punjáb by the aid of modern names, but of course conjecturally.

augur that a greater blessing will attend our arms, than attended his, and greater benefit to the country, which we have subdued.

As we were at breakfast this morning, we heard the firing of cannon in the direction of Lahore, which from its irregularity sounded like battle-firing more than that of a salute, and which therefore was thought to indicate that the Seekh army reinforced was not far off, and that we were on the point of a fifth engagement. The Governor-General said, however, "that we had better finish our breakfast before we went at them." We have heard no more firing since, and it has proved to be a false alarm: it was the firing of a salute at Lahore. Our breakfast tent is very diminutive, just large enough for eight or ten to squeeze into. This is the only tent the Governor-General has to occupy now-a-days in the morning for about three hours, until his double-poled tent comes up; and yesterday morning, after his arrival at the ground, he was obliged to sit for a considerable length of time in his *palkee gáree* (ʰ) writing on a table fixed in the middle of it. This breakfast-tent too is the only place, where any breakfast is to be had in our camp; so that we all crowd round it by instinct, and those, who are too late for seats inside, are very glad to get what they can without seats outside.

(ʰ) Palanquin-carriage.

§ 8. CAMP AT LAHORE.

20th.—We arrived this morning at Meeanmeer between two and three miles from the capital of the Punjáb, the site of the Seekh lines; and thus our army is occupying the ground, whence the Seekh army so lately issued forth on their mad expedition with the confident belief, that they should be our destruction. Mr. Currie and the Governor-General's Staff went to-day to the palace and saw the Máharájah placed upon the throne. The city has an imposing appearance from our camp.

21st.—Most of the trades-people of Lahore, hearing of the approach of our army, were seized with a panic and have run away. Strict orders therefore have been given that no European, except of course official persons sent on public business, is to go into or near the city at present, in order that the inhabitants may have time to gain confidence and understand, that we have no intention of plundering them or doing them any injury.

22nd.—(Sunday.)—Divine service in the Governor-General's tent. When was this service ever held before in this part of the world? Congregation small, though, the army being with us, it might have been expected, that our congregation would be larger than usual. Prince Waldemar attended. He has regularly attended, when he has been in our camp. I like what I have seen of him very much.

23rd.—I went with the Governor-General and Staff to see the *Hazooree Bágh*. It is a small garden in a square between the palace and the *Bádsháhee Musjid* and is entered by a gate called *Badámee bágh-ka durwáza.* In the centre is a marble building containing a suite of rooms. The ground is pretty outside the Badámee bágh-ka durwáza. [1] This is not properly one of the gates

[1] On this ground our camp was pitched in 1847.

CAMP AT LAHORE. 83

of the city. Lahore has twelve gates named as follows: Dehlee (*k*) durwaza, Yeckee, Shahreewala, Cashmeree, (*k*) Mustee, Tungsálee (near which is the Mint, where the Nának Sháh rupees are coined), Bhátee, Moree, Loháree, Shahalmee, Mochee, Akhbaree. The fortifications of the city look strong at first sight; the ditch is wide and deep and the walls high; but on closer inspection they appear not so formidable: they are dilapidated in one or two places, and it is obvious that a breach might easily be effected in them. The Bádsháhee Musjid is a fine building and in better preservation, than might have been expected. The religious fury of the Seekhs has covered the country all round outside the walls with the unsightly ruins of mosques, tombs, and Mohummedan buildings of one kind or another. The religion of the Seekhs is said to be a sort of mixture of Hindooism and Mohummedanism, both

(*k*) So one of the gates of Lucknow is called Roomka durwáza, from its looking towards Greece and Turkey (Roumelia); and at Tyre there was ὁ λιμὴν ὁ πρὸς Αἰγυπτει.

of which however they regard as false: they believe in only one God, like the Mohummedans, and again they retain many religious customs of the Hindoos, while they reject the Prophet and use no idols. They are divided into two sects, the followers of *Gooroo Nának* and those of *Gooroo Govind*. Their sacred book is called *Grunth*. [1] Gooroo Nának or Bába Nának or Nának Sháh was the founder of the Seekh religion. He was born A. D. 1469. He was a Hindoo. His father was of the military caste, and he refused to follow his father's employment, and devoted himself to religion, and travelled into every part of the East, and conversed with persons of all ranks, even with the emperor Báber. The great doctrine he taught was the unity of God; and he strove to convince both Hindoos and Mohummedans of their respective errors. In conjunction with about twelve others he composed the *Purána Grunth*. Gooroo Govind was a descendant of his and was born A. D. 1675. He abolished Hindoo caste among the Seekhs and

[1] *Grunth* is a Sanskrit word signifying "a book."

CAMP AT LAHORE. 85

promoted sweepers to honour. He changed the name Seekh to *Singh* (or lion) and made all his followers soldiers. He composed by himself the *Náya Grunth*. It is written in *Goormoockee*, the written dialect of the sect. The Seekhs admit any one into their religion and into their temples, but for the latter the shoes must be taken off. They are desperate fanatics, like the Mohummedans, and fight against us as infidels and God's enemies; but they are about the most wicked race on the earth and are described as being worse, if possible, than the inhabitants of Sodom and Gomorrah. For murder, rapine, cruelty, licentiousness, beastly lewdness, debauchery of every kind and description, they are not to be surpassed, I imagine, if equalled, by any tribe now living on the face of the globe.

24*th*.—The Seekhs have a very different cast of countenance from that of any other natives: they look like a distinct race. Many see a resemblance in their visages to the Jewish physiognomy. Their long black beards give them an imposing appearance, and some of the soldiers are remarkably fine looking men. The rest of the population of the Punjáb, who form the great majority, are called by the common name of Punjábees, some being Hindoos and others Mohummedans. The latter have been most oppressed by the Seekhs. To what race the people of the Punjáb belong, or where they came from, is unknown. But it is singular that they call themselves *Jats* or *Jeets* or *Juts*, as do also the natives of Scinde. Some think there must be an identity between this word and *Getæ*, as likewise between Getæ and *Gothi* (or Goths). Some however think that the Jats were all originally Hindoos. It is also deserving of remark, in connection with the idea of the Jewish extraction of the Seekhs, that the same idea has been entertained with regard to the Scindians in consequence of their strikingly Jewish features. And the " Adventurer in the Punjáb " tells us, that " the ruler of Baháwalpore and his clan distinguish themselves by the term *dáudputras*, sons of David, from Dáud, *David*, and putra, *a son*, tracing their pedigree to an ancestor in Scinde, whence they emigrated about 100 years ago."—We know very little as yet of this part of the world and its people, and a wide field is open for ethnological investigation; but the connection of these tribes with Israel in some way or other is quite obvious. Lady Sale again in p. 283 of her journal says, "We passed over the plain of Methusaleh and saw at a short distance the Kubber-i-Lámech, a celebrated place of pilgrimage about 2 miles from Tighree and 25 from Jellalabad." In an interesting book, called "Our Israelitish origin," the Author, Mr. Wilson, makes out that the Goths, i. q. Getæ, were Israelites. But it is to be hoped that we shall prosecute our researches into the history of these parts and their population, now that Providence seems about to afford us every possible facility for the purpose.(*)

(*) See Prichard's Researches, vol. iv. p. 239. Wiseman's Lectures on the Connection between Science and

25th.—(Ash Wednesday.)—No Church-bell to-day. Nor do I think that the Governor-General is to be blamed for not ordering Service. "I will have mercy and not sacrifice," surely applies on such occasions as these, if ever it did at all. A friend told me to-day that in the Commander-in-Chief's camp Service is held twice every Sunday. The Commander-in-Chief has no Chaplain, but Colonel Eckford officiates. I hear that the Loo-diána Missionaries (they are Americans) have been privately recommended by a friend of theirs, a member of our own Church, to lose no time in taking measures for the establishment of a Mission on this side of the Sutlej in our newly acquired Jullunder territory.

Revealed Religion, Lect. viii. Paganism and Christianity compared by Dr. Ireland, ch. iii.—Major Abbott, in the Essay above referred to, speaks of the resemblance of the Kuttris, a race of people widely diffused through the Punjáb, to the Jews of Asia in feature, dress, and customs; and also alleges, as evidence of the Israelitish descent of the Affghans, the identity of some Mosaic and Affghan names and the mention of them by Greek writers 1000 years before the Hejira.

CAMP AT LAHORE. 89

27*th*.—I accompanied the Commander-in-Chief's party to see the Shálamáh gardens about 2 miles to the east of the city. They are like all other oriental gardens, that I have seen; exceedingly stiff, mathematically formal, with paved walks. The trees are chiefly mango-trees, the flowers, stocks and larkspur and red poppies. The reservoir and the summer-houses, &c. are of white marble, Mohummedan in style and structure. We were regaled with oranges as hard as bullets and tasteless as turnips. Upon the whole our visit to these famous gardens was repaid by disappointment.

It is by no means safe to go about alone far beyond the limits of the camp. The Seekhs in the city and villages round are still as insolent as possible ; and, inasmuch as they are practised ruffians and cut-throats, they are not pleasant people for a lonely Faringee to meet with. The other day a poor European soldier, straggling too far from camp, was fallen upon by a set of savages and literally hacked and chopped to death.

Another day two Sipáhees went into the city (the prohibition against going there being no longer in force) and came back severely cut with sabres. The Seekhs are very far from being subdued in spirit; and it is very possible they may rise again next winter or the winter after and give us some more work.

28*th.*—Two Pundits ([n]) out of the city called on me yesterday and asked for a religious book to read. I gave them a copy of St. John's Gospel in Hindee and a tract on "the evil of sin." They said they would come again to-day; but they have not come. We had some refreshing showers of rain to-day; but nothing less than 48 hours of incessant rain would be enough to lay the dust in this part of the world.

March 1*st.*—(Sunday.)—Divine Service in the Governor-General's tent; large congregation. The Commander-in-Chief and Staff attended, the Commander-in-Chief sitting at the table on the right of the Governor-General. After Service an

([n]) Learned Brahmans.

old Cánpoor friend called at my tent, and we had a long conversation on religious matters: a great refreshment and a very rare one. One of the Officers of our camp went out this morning to spend the day with some pleasure-party at the Shálamáh Gardens: this is the way to recommend our religion to the heathen.

2nd.—The Pundit came according to his promise and brought along with him three of his adult disciples. He said he did not want to know anything about the Christian religion, and that the books which I had given him were not what he required. I told him something about heathenism and about the true God and bade him read the Gospel I had given him; but I could elicit nothing from him, except a Satanic laugh.

3rd.—Men are going about with old coins to sell. They are of gold, silver and brass, with Greek devices and inscriptions. Major Macdonald tells me that there are Jews in Cábul, who are very clever in counterfeiting the ancient Greek and Bactrian coins, which are found in these parts of the country, and that therefore there is some risk in buying what are carried about for sale.

I went this morning in company with three Officers to see the city. We were recommended to go on elephants, that we might suffer the less inconvenience from the extreme filthiness of the streets; and we were not sorry afterwards that we followed the advice. The streets are just wide enough to admit an elephant—there is no room for a horse to pass him. A nasty gutter runs through the middle of each street. The people seem to live in filth and to rejoice, like pigs, in mire and stench. The houses are built of *pukka* (º) brick, and are several stories high with stairs inside. The doors, window-frames, and shutters, are made of hard-looking wood and covered with ornamental carving. All the inhabitants of this Sodom, men and women alike, have a sinister and diabolical expression of countenance. Many of the men look the more

(º) Hard, well-baked.

unearthly from having lost one eye or their noses or ears, a mutilation inflicted on them for some offence. They have a most independent and impudent appearance; their shops are busy still with the making and sharpening of swords, &c., as if they calculated on being a match for us yet. As we passed along, almost every window was filled with prostitutes, disgusting, sickly, wanton-looking objects, decked out in the livery of their profession. From all I hear and read of the depravity of this place, I should suppose a virtuous woman in Lahore would be a *rara avis*. This however is nothing: a Hindoo once told me that he believed such a person would be a rarity in any town of Hindoostán. (*p*) But it

(*p*) The prostitution of females however *is* worse in the Punjáb than elsewhere. For the Author of the "Adventurer in the Punjáb" says that it is more licentious and more extensive there, than anywhere else. It is not only legalized, but parents are systematically murdered for the sake of obtaining the girls to make a trade of. I take this opportunity of expressing my unqualified disgust at the opinion of those, who consider that female prostitution is more excusable in countries, where it is legalized and where it is the crime of Sodom, which, though common throughout the East, is awfully prevalent here, that gives to Lahore the preeminence in wickedness. To this also must be added wholesale murder and drunkenness.

I understand that there are no Jews in Lahore. There were a few some years ago, but they have all left.

March 4*th.*—To-day I was again refreshed by some religious conversation with an Officer, whose acquaintance I made at Simla, whom I believe to be a sincere Christian. Alas! how rare are such jewels! Whatever their number may be, I feel sure, from my own observation and experience, that it must be *comparatively* very small and insignificant.

Sir C. Napier arrived yesterday. When he

is not viewed as a sin. It is so much the worse for being legalized in *any* country. It is sanctioned in France, which is a *Christian* country. The people mentioned in Gen. vi. 2, had no better means of knowing that fornication was a sin, than heathens have in the present day; and yet it is represented to have been the chief cause of the deluge.

was directed to join the army, it was not expected that the war would be over so soon.

5th.—The Governor-General gave a grand dinner. I should think all the Officers of the Army were present. The Commander-in-Chief sat on his right hand, Sir C. Napier on his left. The dinner was immediately followed by toasts and speeches, in which the veteran *triumviri* just mentioned took the most conspicuous part. Each eulogized the other and the army at large. I wonder what the native attendants think of our deafening "Hip, hip, hip, hurrahs!"

Sir C. Napier is one of the most remarkable-looking men I ever beheld: Short in stature, of a thin cadaverous visage, with a fine aquiline nose, strongly marked eye-brows, eyes of a hawk behind a huge pair of spectacles, dark brown hair and a long gray beard. He is fluent in speech and his voice sepulchral. I can readily understand how at first sight some of his fellow-men have considered him to belong to other than earthly regions. He is called by the natives of

Scinde "*Shytán-ka bháee.*"(*q*) The designation, however, may be also perhaps ascribable to the wonderfully short work which he made with his enemies in that region.

8th.—(Sunday.)—Divine Service, as usual; large congregation. Sir C. Napier attended, sitting on the left of the Governor-General, and the Commander-in-Chief on the right.

9th.—The Governor-General held a large durbár for the reception of the Máharájah and the ratification of the treaty. The Governor-General was seated on his throne with the Máharájah on another throne on his right and Prince Waldemar on his left. The *Sáhib lóg* (*r*) were ranged on one side of the tent, the *Sirdár lóg* (*r*) on the other. The Governor-General's band played at intervals outside. The Governor-General explained in the audience of all present the conduct, the wishes, and intentions, of the British Government with regard to the Government of Lahore. Mr.

(*q*) Satan's brother.
(*r*) The British Officers—The Seekh Chiefs.

Currie interpreted the Governor-General's words to the Seekh Chiefs sentence by sentence. The treaty was signed; and the business concluded with the distribution of *nuzzurs* (*) to the value, I heard, of 30,000 rupees.

There was a large dinner-party at the Commander-in-Chief's tent with toasts and speeches, the *anti-strophe* to the *strophe* of the 5th.

This treaty is looked upon by many as a thing patched up for present expediency, to be broken by the Seekhs the first opportunity. It strikes me however that this is the first step to our sovereign possession of the Punjáb. Rájah Gooláb Singh is to have Cashmere and to be independent of the Lahore Government, and to keep an army of his own. Cashmere no doubt will be ours too at some future day. O that the Gospel could be preached for a witness to the miserable people of that beautiful vale! Gooláb's countenance is the picture of astuteness. I dare say, when he is perfectly at ease in his new dominion, it will

(*) Presents.

be also the picture of lust and cruelty, for which he is equally notorious. I believe that one of his favourite punishments is that of flaying alive.(¹)

10*th*.—A durbár was held at the palace by the Máharájah for the reception of the Governor-General. The elegant room or hall of audience, in which it was held, is certainly well worth seeing. The front of it, which is open, forms one side or nearly so of a quadrangle, in the middle of which is a reservoir of water with a jet d'eau. The room is entered from this side under arches of white marble and from the opposite or interior side by a door leading into the private apartments of the palace. The roof and walls are spangled with inlaid work of

---

(¹) This is the amiable creature, of whom the Frenchman says, " C'est un homme d'une beauté extrême et des manières les plus simples, les plus douces et les plus élégantes,"—and again on parting from his friend, " J'ai quitté avant-hier, le rajah Goulab-Sing, enchanté de lui comme il l'était de moi."—Correspondance de Victor Jacquemont, Tome ii., p. 2, 7. The etymological meaning of Goolab Singh is *rose-water lion*.

various-coloured glass or stone. From the roof are suspended European chandeliers; and at each end is fixed a large oblong mirror, these likewise reminding one of Europe. The floor is carpeted with Cashmere shawls; and a canopy outside, lined with Cashmere shawls, protects the inside from the sun. Shawls too were strewed upon the ground of the quadrangle, but this I presume was only for the occasion. The *Sirdár lóg* were all in their best attire, and the variety of costume presented a showy spectacle. There was no business to be done at this durbár: it was a mere idle ceremony. The *koh-i-noor* (") or great diamond, about the size of a pigeon's egg, was exhibited to the company; and the presentation of shawls and swords concluded the *tamásha*.(')

11*th*.—I went to breakfast with Dr. Hoffingberger, a German Surgeon, who has been residing in Lahore for many years as a manufacturer of gunpowder for Seekh guns and also of medicine for Seekh stomachs. As things have turned out,

(") Mountain of Light.   (') Show.

he has put more to death by the former trade, than he has saved alive by the latter. The gunpowder trade however is now exploded, and my friend must complete his fortune by powder from the doctor's shop. I went for the purpose of complying with a request, which he made, that I should baptize his children; for the performance of which office I never saw any one so grateful.(*) Colonel Mouton was there, a

(*) By such cases one is reminded of primitive and apostolic times; and what a contrast do they present to the unbecoming behaviour of so many, especially among the upper classes of our countrymen, who, as though from the very commonness and accessibility of the Sacraments and other public means of grace, do not feel their value; and who seem to regard them as matters of course, or as rights to be demanded, instead of favours to be thankful for, and the Officers of the Church as their own servants to do their bidding instead of servants of Christ; and who make the baptism of their children, what certainly neither Scripture nor the Prayer Book makes it, a mere form, or an occasion for carnal conviviality instead of spiritual joy! When Chaplain of a station, where no hindrance has existed to the regular observance of the Rubrick, I have known members of our Church, very gay members of " society,"

French Officer, late of the Seekh service. By the result of the war this Officer's prospects here are blighted: he is about to return to his native land. Yes, Colonel Mouton, we have beaten the Seekhs, even though they were trained by Officers from *la grande nation.*

as the term is, positively appeal to the Bishop of the Diocese against me and indignantly complain, because they have been told that Sundays and holy days are the days appointed for the public administration of infant baptism; and I have known an Officer prohibit a non-commissioned Officer under his command from taking his child to the Church for baptism, rather than that he should submit to the intolerable hardship of having his infant christened on a Sunday: the fact having been in each case, that the only objection to Sunday has been the unsuitableness of the day for balls and carousals.

§ 9. DEPARTURE FROM LAHORE.

THE Governor-General's camp left Lahore this evening. A large force is to remain for the protection of the Máharájah's Government; the rest of the Army is to return to our own provinces. All is quiet at present and there is no immediate prospect of peace being interrupted. Oh what a change have we witnessed in the fortunes of that great city! May the blessings of peace and order, truth and justice, be established henceforth within thy walls! And may the day be at hand, when the light of Revelation shall penetrate into thy dark recesses of impurity and wretchedness, and the word of the living God be preached for a testimony to all thy people! O thou bloody city! The voice of the blood, which thou hast shed, and of the crimes, which thou hast perpetrated, crieth from the ground and will cry against thee in the day of judgment. But for thy future generations there is hope—there is hope that they may hear the glad tidings of other Blood, which has been shed for thee and can change thee from the filthiness of thine iniquity so soon as thou shalt believe the report.

We marched to *Shálamáh Bágh*. Sir C. Napier accompanied us to this place; he takes his leave to-morrow morning for his own province. I have not observed anything eccentric in his manner; he is gentlemanly, affable, and even deferential in society; and there appears nothing strange about him, except his physiognomy. The *bágh* was put in trim and shown off to its best advantage for the occasion of its being visited by the Governor-General; the fountains were set playing, and the whole was enlivened by the music of one of our bands, who stood upon a marble platform in the middle of a reservoir of water. The Seekhs appear to be fond of flower-gardens: there are several on a smaller scale in the neighbourhood of Lahore. But the formality of an oriental garden is not agreeable to an English eye.

12*th.—Pull,* 10 miles. The distance that a newborn camel can walk is perfectly astonishing: when three or even two days old, it can walk five miles; when four days, seven miles. A cameldriver, in whose charge I observed a very young camel trudging along by the side of its mother, gave me this information.

13*th.—Bhopoora,* 10 miles.

14*th.—Umritsir,* 10½ miles. This is a large town, the most strongly fortified in the Punjáb, and, I suppose, next to Lahore, the dirtiest. The fort is called Govindgurh. Its chief strength consists in the depth and width of the ditch. But I believe it has one fault: a great deal of the building inside is conspicuous from without, whereas the science of fortification requires that nothing of the interior should be a visible object for the enemy to fire at. Umritsir(*), the meaning

(*) *Umrit*, ambrosia, and *sir*, head.

of which is "fountain-head of holiness," is the stronghold of the Seekh religion. The holy tank is here, in the middle of which is the marble shrine, where the holy book or *Grunth Sáhib* is kept under the perpetual charge of a chief Gooroo and worshipped by crowds daily, not only by the inhabitants of the town, but by pilgrims from all parts. The expression of the countenances of these Gooroos is that of indescribable *hauteur*. Here too the Akálees or "immortals" reside within the precincts of the holy tank. These are frantic demoniacs, and it is very dangerous to go near them. They are distinguished by a fiendish look, blue turbans, long dishevelled hair, and small iron things like horse-shoes stuck about their head-dress, which they use to fling at people; and they also carry a short club for the purpose, I believe, of throwing at a Faringee or any one that the devil incites them against. These demoniacs possess an awful influence over the people, being regarded as demi-gods; and when any public emergency arises, a convocation of Akálees is held at Umritsir, and whatever they decree is considered to be the voice of heaven and acted upon with universal enthusiasm. But I imagine that there is an end of them now, and that these holy synods will only be spoken of in the past tense.

The Seekhs will admit any one into their religion. The ceremony of initiation is called *pahul* and is remarkable: water is sprinkled upon the convert, and at the same time a kind of sweetmeat called *batása*, cut into square bits, with wine is administered to him. The ceremony must be performed by five or more Seekhs together in any place, no matter where, in doors or out. One of them reads to the neophyte the canons of faith. His initiation is then complete and he is become a μύστης. He then chooses a Gooroo for himself, to give him further instruction, that he may become an ἐπόπτης.(*y*)

(*y*) An American Missionary, who has been among them, has since told me that the Seekhs have also a *periodical* breaking and distribution of bread in token of their religious union and brotherhood.

DEPARTURE FROM LAHORE. 107

Most of the houses in Umritsir are painted all over with figures of men, women, beasts and birds, among which the sacred peacock predominates. Some of the figures are very obscene.

This place is famous for its attar of roses and for its shawls. The latter are inferior to the Cashmere shawls, though made by Cashmerees who reside here, and said to be of the same materials. They say the inferiority is in the dye of the thread. But I suspect the manufacture is not precisely the same: they acknowledge that an Umritsir shawl will not last a quarter of the time that a Cashmere one will; and the price of the former is not above a quarter of the price of the latter.

The Governor-General held a durbár for the reception of the monster, Rájah Gooláb Singh.

15*th*.—(Sunday).—Divine Service, as usual; small congregation. There had been a heavy fall of rain; the rain however had subsided at 11 o'clock, the hour of Service, nor did it prevent any from going out for their own pleasure.

16th. — Lord Elphinstone, late Governor of Madras, joined our camp a few days ago, as Aide-de-Camp to the Governor-General. This afternoon two men came to my tent selling attar of roses and other things manufactured here. I gave them some tracts in Hindoostánee, which they said they could read. In the evening I went to the durbár given by Gooláb Singh to the Governor-General at the house of Téj Singh, a short distance from the fort; and thence to Ram Bágh, a garden made by Runjeet Singh, in which garden there is nothing worth seeing. From the top of Téj Singh's house there is a fine view of the surrounding country, which, though flat, is beautiful at this time of year, when the crops of corn are full grown. The wheat grows three or four feet high, bearded as in Hindoostán. The rain has made the weather delightful: no temperature on earth could be more delightful than this, which we have enjoyed to-day. Gooláb Singh has a remarkable fine and handsome set of men about him, as his body-guards: they are Kohistánees. The

DEPARTURE FROM LAHORE. 109

Seekh way of firing a salute is very different from ours: they fire with no regularity and as quick as as they can.

17th.—*Cung*, 14 miles. The country all along very fertile, covered with fine crops of wheat and gram. We passed by a singular conical mound of earth, looking at a distance like a small pyramid. The villagers could not or would not tell us what it was made for.

18th.—*Subdulpoor*, 7 miles. Here we crossed the Beeas or Hyphasis.(*) It is a large stream even at this season of the year. Two bridges of boats had been constructed for our passage similar to those over the Sutlej at Ferozepoor, only that the boats here were country affairs and most ridiculous objects. We have managed therefore better than the Macedonian hero, who was obliged to make the same bridge serve for the Indus and

(*) Some suppose that not the Beeas or Beyah, but the river Ghurra, formed by the junction of the Beeas and the Sutlej, was the ancient Hyphasis. Still the derivation of Beeas from Upasis or Hyphasis, Ύφασις, can scarcely be doubted.

Hydaspes, and to have the boats cut into pieces and conveyed across the country from one river to the other.(*a*) The Beeas is the new boundary of our North-West frontier; so that this morning we encamped on our own ground and consequently feel more at home. The crops of wheat on both sides of the river are luxuriant.

19*th*. — *Sultanpoor*, 11 miles. We passed through a continued succession of corn-fields. It would be impossible for the ground to be more richly covered than it is. In some places the wheat was four or five feet high; whereas in Hindoostan the straw of the wheat has always struck me as being very short and stunted. So far as we have seen, we have no reason to be dissatisfied with our newly-acquired territory.

In all these villages or towns, that we pass through, the houses are chiefly built of small pukka bricks, the best of them ornamented outside with figures of birds, and the walls painted with various mythological or other ridiculous devices.

(*a*) See an amusing account of this in Arrian, v. 8.

DEPARTURE FROM LAHORE. 111

I cannot help remarking the elaborate carving of the doors and window-frames and shutters, for which these people seem to have a great fancy: even in the smallest village there is some of it.

We came to-day through the village of *Tulwundi*, the birthplace of Bába Nának, founder of the Seekh religion, deluded author of delusion. What associations rise in one's mind! What a contrast between Tulwundi and Bethlehem!

20*th.*—*Deccanikee Sarai*, 14 miles. This district is the property of Bába Bikram, a lineal descendant of Nának. A beautifully clear brook, which is a rare thing in the plains of India, is to be seen at this place.

21*st.*—*Nurmahl*, 10 miles.

22*nd.*—*Philór*, 10 miles. The British flag is an interesting object floating on the top of the fort, which surrendered after the battle of Alliwál. This memorable spot is about 12 miles farther down the river. Philór is close upon the Sutlej, which is a wide stream here even now. Sirdár

Runjoor Singh crossed over here with his forces and burned some of the public buildings at Loodiána, for which they received condign punishment at Alliwál from Sir H. Smith.

This day is Sunday, but the Governor-General thought it necessary to march. He went yesterday to Jullunder by another road and joined the camp this morning. I understand that his object in marching to-day is to save time and hasten to the hills, as the weather is becoming oppressively warm. We had Divine Service in the afternoon.(*b*)

23rd.—Loodiána, 6 miles. We crossed the Sutlej by a bridge of boats. This station is all sand, the sister of Ferozepoor, which is all dust.

So much for the Campaign of 1845-6.

(*b*) Philór is conjectured by Major James Abbott to be the spot, where Alexander's progress was arrested, and where he built twelve altars as memorials of his own exploits and for thanksgiving to the gods. See *Journal of the Asiatic Society of Bengal*, No. iii., 1852, " On the sites of Nikaia and Boukephalon;" also Arrian, v., 29 ; Q. Curtius, ix., 3; Strabo, iii., 171. If so, our happening to be there on the Lord's day and offering a service and worship so different on the same spot was a remarkable coincidence.

PART II.

TOUR IN THE PUNJAB AND UPPER PROVINCES IN 1846-7.

§ 1.

OCT. 31*st*, 1846.—Camp, *Kalka*. I left Simla on the 29th inst. to join the camp for another marching tour. The Governor-General has gone a different route through the hills viâ Belaspoor, intending to join the camp at Hoshearpoor about the end of next month. Between Simla and Kalka are three bunglas for the accommodation of travellers, but how different from English hotels! Still they are better than nothing; and how travellers contrived before the Hon. Company's staging bunglas were erected, I am at a loss to conceive. In the largest of the bunglas on the road down to this place there are only four rooms, in the others only two. If these rooms be occupied, the only alternative is to sleep outside. This was my unfortunate case at Hurreepoor, where on arrival I found the bungla full. I put up for the night in the stable between two horses, certainly a rude kind of dormitory, having neither doors nor the fraction of a door, swarming with rats, and in point of odour very different from "the perfumed chambers of the great;" yet I slept, and "nature's soft nurse" was more efficient there, than under many "canopies of costly state;" and I remembered that the King of kings "was laid in a manger, because there was no room for them in the inn." Captain Peel, Aide-de-Camp to the Governor-General, wrapped himself in his cloak and reposed for the night upon the bare ground outside in the open air. The coolies are a whole day in bringing up our luggage; so that I must be content with one meal a day, either early in the morning or late at night. This rough work however only lasts for three days, till we join the camp at the foot of the hills. I do not feel the change of temperature much, though by the thermometer it is great. At Simla on the 28th inst. the thermometer stood at noon in the shade at 63° Fahr., to-day it is 81°. We have two accessions to our camp-society, one a civilian, the other a military officer; the latter apparently a clever man. But no man can be spiritually minded, that uses the name of God in vain.

Nov. 1*st.* — Divine Service was held in the morning. There were only five attendants besides the men and boys of the Governor-General's band, who are *ordered* to attend. Four others might have attended, if they had chosen, for they were quite well and about all day. Those, who were present, did not once kneel down—the posture enjoined by the Prayer-book and by Scripture and by the very highest Example, the observance or non-observance of which posture is very significant of the frame of mind—if the spirit pray, the body must and will pray with it. But why did none of the officers of the Body-guard and of the 73rd Regiment N. I. in escort make their appearance?

I fear the reason may be found in Rom. viii. 7. Knowing that it is arranged to march next Sunday, and knowing that there is no necessity for such arrangement, I alluded in my sermon to the sin of unnecessary travelling on the Lord's day. No hearts are too hard for God to turn, unless they be reprobate.

2nd.—Pinjore, 4 miles. Here is a beautiful garden belonging to the Rájah of Puttiála, which is the name of this district. He was the only Rájah of the Seekh states that stood our firm ally during the late war. This garden, like the Shálamáh garden at Lahore, consists of several terraces one above another, and appears to cover as much ground. But the tanks and summer-houses are not built of marble, as those in the Shálamáh. A canal of water runs through the middle of the garden, broken by several beautifully-constructed artificial cataracts, and ornamented with *jets d'eau* at frequent and regular intervals all the way down, and kept in excellent order. These were all set playing on occasion of our arrival. The water is conveyed here by an aqueduct from the hills. Waterfalls like these over smooth wide edges are called by the natives *páneekee chádur*, which is literally "a sheet of water"—a remarkable coincidence of idiom. In the evening the garden was lighted up with numberless little lamps of oil: a man told me that 30 maunds, *i. e.*, 2,400 lbs. of oil were spent in the illumination. The lamps were placed all round the borders of the water and in the wall behind the cascades, producing a thoroughly magic effect, and round the edges of the summit of the gateway and the summer-houses. The moon also shining brightly made the scene still more romantic. I saw in this garden a row of what I do not remember having observed in India before, but what struck me as being poplar-trees, though smaller than they grow in England.

3rd.—*Munnamájra*, 8 miles. A pretty spot. A Rájah resides here. In the middle of the town is a half-famished tiger in a large cage.

4th.—*Khurrur*, 12 miles. The whole of the

road heavy sand. Mornings and evenings cold, noon very warm. I have dined to-day with Captain Harrison, our new commissariat-officer, who seems to be a religious man.

5th.—Bussee, 14½ miles. Road all sand, if it can be called a road : we are going across country. We started this morning at half-past three o'clock, by beautiful moonlight, and arrived at sunrise. Thermometer at noon 79°. One of the drummers of the 73rd Regiment N. I., came to my tent to ask me for a Prayer-Book. From his conversation I hope he is an exception to his class ; the Christian musicians attached to the native regiments being generally very vicious and depraved. I gave him some tracts. I have bought to-day, as a curiosity, a large bag knitted of worsted of various dyes, a manufacture of this place.

6th.—Kunnahkee Sarái, 13 miles. Very hot. This morning I was talking with a member of the camp about the spiritual character of certain persons, and I mentioned to him one of them that we both knew to have led a vicious life. My friend said that I should be surprised, if I knew the extent, to which the vice I referred to (illicit intercourse with native women) is looked upon as venial in this country by Englishmen; and he told me that he once heard a Judge pronounce it his opinion, that the question of veniality was very different between such intercourse with European, *i. e.* Christian, and with native, *i. e.* heathen women, the criminality being less in the latter case, because prostitution is not considered criminal by the natives, but is a recognised and respected professional means of livelihood. Righteous judgment to be decreed by a Christian judge! My friend remarked, that he himself thought there was less amount of guilt in the case of native women. But I must differ from him: surely the guilt is no less, because the conscience is hardened and the practice inveterate; the sin is the same in God's sight, who for the prevalence of fornication destroyed the world with a flood; who listens to no excuses, regards no customs, and frowns, if possible, even more severely upon a Christian joining himself to a heathen, than upon the same joining himself to a Christian harlot.

7th. — *Dowrahkee Sarái*, 13 miles. Heavy sandy road. We passed that famous place, *Lushkur khankee Sarái*, where we were encamped last December.

8th.—(Sunday.)—Divine Service was held in the morning in the Governor-General's tent. In the evening I summoned the Christian drummers and fifers of the 73rd Regiment to Hindoostánee prayers in my tent; though Hindoostánee service is unsatisfactory, because the congregation have no books and their attention is unfixed.(*c*) We were to have marched on this day, but I am glad to find that the arrangement has been altered. The 4th Light Cavalry, under a British officer of course, on their way to the Jullunder Dooáb, encamped here yesterday, but proceeded to-day

(*c*) The Benáres translation of the Book of Common Prayer into Oordoo was not then published. It ought to be possessed by all native and Eurasian Christians able to read.

on their march. I believe there was no necessity whatever for this non-observance of the 4th *Commandment* by the *commanding* officer.

9th.—Loodiána, 14 miles. What melancholy vestiges are here of the barracks of Her Majesty's 50th Regiment, which were blown down a short time ago by a storm, and buried upwards of eighty bodies in their ruins!

10th.—A Seekh infantry corps is being raised here; they are remarkably fine looking men; most, if not all, of them six feet high, and some more. The bazaar-people describe them as being very independent and *zubburdust* (violent). My friend, Captain Wake, is here with his regiment. I dined with him this evening, and met Major Wheeler of the same corps, who is a very religious man, and takes great interest in the conversion of the natives to the Christian faith, and reads and talks to them in Hindoostánee and distributes religious tracts amongst them. Very angry to-day with my Christian servant, John Field: he goes out to his acquaintances among the Christian drummers and fifers of the Native Infantry Regiments, drinks and comes back impertinent.

11th.—Philore, 9 miles, *i. e.* to *the Station*. A healthy, pretty spot. The fort is a picturesque object, and the river still more so. Several bunglas have been erected, and the roads cut out. Thermometer at noon in the shade 79°. A Punjábee workman came to my tent to-day to do a little work; and I was struck with the humble, contented manner, in which he took what I paid him for it: for a Hindoostánee would perhaps have scarcely said "Thank you." He was almost naked. I asked him why he had no clothes on; he said that the poor people in the Punjáb have been accustomed to wear no clothes because of the Seekhs, who used to rob them of everything, and would have stripped their clothes off them, if they had worn any. Riding out in the evening, I met another poor man working in a field and cutting *sun* (hemp, *cannabis sativa*), of the stalks of which they make string and ropes; and he too gave me a similar account of their oppression by the Seekhs, who used to come to their villages and plunder *ad libitum*, and make the poor villagers themselves carry the plunder for them in loads on their heads, threatening to cut off their noses, &c., if they resisted. Thanks be to God, the righteous judge and avenger of the oppressed, vengeance has overtaken the tyrants, and the pit, which they dug for others, they have fallen into the midst of it themselves.

> ἀντὶ δὲ πληγῆς φονίας φονίαν
> πληγὴν τινέτω. Δράσαντι παθεῖν
> τριγέρων μῦθος τάδε φωνεῖ.
>
> Æsch. Choeph. 309.

"The Lord hath arisen against the house of the evil-doers, and against the help of them that work iniquity." Is. xxxi. 2.

12th.—Phugwára, 14 miles. We have been struck with the shortness of the distances and their generally appearing less than stated by the Quartermaster; but in to-day's march I am sure there was no mistake; not that I would reflect at all on the accuracy of the Quartermaster's measurement as to the marches of other days; the mistake or deception must be in ourselves. We usually start at 3 or 4 o'clock in the morning, which is not unpleasant, for it is cool and moonlight; and we are enabled to arrive about sunrise, and our baggage comes up about 9 o'clock. This morning, however, I did not arrive till 8, and my luggage not till half-past ten. The fields appear to be in a good state of cultivation. This Jullunder Dooáb is celebrated as the most fertile part of the Punjáb. All the poor people, men, women and children, come out of their houses, as we pass through the villages, to have a stare at their new masters. They look pleased, so at least I fancy. That they have cause indeed to be pleased already at the change of their rulers, there can be no doubt. They are no longer oppressed nor plundered. Everyone must acknowledge the wisdom of the Governor-General in attending without loss of time to the civil administration of the territory, and thus conciliating the people to our rule; nor could he well have appointed a more suitable man for this work than Mr. John Lawrence, Civil Service, brother of Colonel Lawrence, the founder of the Hill Asylum. (*d*)

Nothing worth seeing here, except a walled garden of ancient date, in the middle of which is a square summer-house, elaborately painted inside, all over the walls and ceiling, with flowers and figures: it has twelve door-ways or entrances, three on each side, and hence this kind of place is called *bárah-dur-ee*.

13*th.—Kanoora*, 15 miles, as measured by our Quartermaster.

(*d*) Called "The Lawrence Asylum," after its benevolent founder and munificent benefactor. It is built at one of the stations in the Himalayas, and its object is to receive for education the children of European soldiers, instead of their being brought up at Regimental schools in the heat of the plains, and under the impure influence of a barrack-life. Like every good cause, this excellent institution had at first great opposition to contend against; but it is now in a flourishing condition. It is superintended by a clergyman of the Church of England.

14th.—*Hoshiarpoor*, 10 miles, *i. e.*, to our camp, which is in the cantonments, and 5 miles from the town. A pretty spot, not far from the foot of a range of hills tipped with snow. They say it is cool here all the year round. Several bunglas have been erected and soldiers' huts for three companies of the 72nd Regiment N. I. I dined this evening with Capt. Harrison, and met two other members of the camp. One of the company had the peculiar faculty of falling asleep with his cigar (an almost inseparable appendage to himself) in his mouth, and yet at the same time being alive to everything said by the others present.

15th.—(Sunday.)—Divine Service in the morning in the Governor-General's tent. Scarcely any of the congregation kneel. I suppose they think it is *infra dignitatem,* or too much trouble, to "fall low on their knees before the footstool" of the Divine Majesty.

17th.—This evening I rode on an elephant to the town. The road and the country are pretty; but much of the plain bears signs of being inundated during the rainy season. The town, like all others in this part of the world, consists of narrow filthy streets and irregular dingy buildings, with a Sirdar's house or a temple here and there towering above the rest. The people look dissolute. The place abounds with prostitutes decked out in gaudy attire and soliciting the wages of sin. The date-tree flourishes here in great abundance. The myrobalan also grows here, called by the natives *hur* or *hurra*, which they say is good for the stomach-ache. Sugar-cane is much cultivated in this neighbourhood.

19*th*.—This morning I rode to Hoshiarpoor to see the fort: there is nothing to see, but 13 guns on carriages, 11 of brass, 2 of iron, some of them apparently very ancient. What an interesting curiosity for the British Museum would be the first great gun that was ever made! We do not know for certain when such weapons of war were invented. It is commonly said that ordnance was first used at the battle of Cressy in 1346; but Lord Bacon maintains that it was employed by the

Oxidraces in India and was what the Macedonians called thunder and lightning and magic; (*) and both gunpowder and ordnance appear to have been used in China from a date still more remote. Some suppose that the use of cannon by Mohummed II., at the siege of Constantinople, is foretold in the Book of Revelation—" By these three was the third part of men killed, by the fire and by the smoke and by the brimstone, which issued out of their mouths." ix. 18.

21st.—The Governor-General arrived in camp this evening.

22nd.—(Sunday.)—Divine Service in Governor-General's tent. There is an Eurasian here of the name of Philips, employed in the Magistrate's office, who distributes religious tracts among the natives and is warmly interested in the great cause of their conversion.

23rd.—To-day I read the burial-service over the body of one of the Governor-General's band, who died of inflammation in the stomach from

(*) *Essays, Civil and Moral,* 58. "Of vicissitude of things."

drinking. The wretched man was an inveterate drunkard. I am told that once he gave up the habit for twelve months, but took to it again. I have known cases, where sobriety or perhaps total abstinence has been maintained for several months, but the habit has always returned; and I have invariably heard officers say, that they have never known a drunkard to be reclaimed. I remember a poor victim of this vice in hospital at Cánpoor declaring to me with tears in his eyes, that the propensity had so mastered him, that temperance pledges were of no avail, and, though he might remain sober for months, he could not shake it off. Sadly striking examples of " serving sin," " obeying sin in the lusts thereof," " sin having dominion over" one, " sin reigning in the mortal body," men "yielding themselves servants of sin unto death!"

I often wish that our Burial-service were altered: to say over the remains of *some*, " as our hope is this our brother doth," is not only painful to the reader, but must have a bad effect upon the hearers. As it is, we commit to the ground with these choice words of Christian comfort the remains of adulterers, fornicators, drunkards, blasphemers, infidels, servants of Mammon, evil-doers and evil-thinkers of every sort and every class, and known to be such to the last. It was not so in the primitive Church.

I passed by a miserable little temple, like a small hovel, with a hole in it by way of entrance just large enough to admit a boy on his hands and knees; and on stooping down to look in, I saw a slab of stone resting against the opposite side with the figure of a snake carved in relief upon it—this is the object of worship. Was there not "a lie in the right hand" of the artificer? and was it not "the Serpent, that beguiled Eve through his subtlety?" How strange, that the snake should be almost universally sacred among heathen nations!

An irregular cavalry corps, commanded by Brevet Captain Quin, and the 36th Regiment N. I., have arrived at this place, which is to be their station.

AND UPPER PROVINCES IN 1846-7. 131

26*th.*—This morning Mr. Currie left for Lahore. What his errand is, I do not exactly know; but it is reported that some intrigue on the part of Lol Singh has been detected, and that Mr. C. has gone to arrange his removal from the *wazeeree*. (*f*)

29*th.*—(Sunday.)—Divine Service in the Governor-General's tent. In the afternoon I collected five of the Governor-General's band into my tent for a lecture; which I mean to continue every Sunday: they are very ignorant. Mr. Philips called on me to-day; he tells me that the *zameendárs*(*g*) and *ráiyuts*(*g*) call themselves Játs; (*h*) also that the Grunthees, or teachers of the Grunth, are much more lukewarm and indifferent than the Pundits (*i*) and the Moulvees (*i*) of Hindoostán.

Dec. 3*rd.*—Thermometer at noon in shade 69°. A few days ago two Seekhs came to my tent and said they were the servants of a Gooroo, and that they

(*f*) The ministry: *wazeer* is a Minister of State.
(*g*) Landholders and tenants.
(*h*) See above p. 86.
(*i*) Learned Brahmans and learned Muhummedans.

wanted to make their *salám* to me. I gave them a tract. To-day they came again and said the tract was very good, and that they should like another for their children; so I gave them another. They tell me they can procure a Grunth for me at Jullunder, where we are going. I understand that the natives here are very anxious to have an English school established, *i. e.*, a school for teaching English. I am also informed that the American missionaries of Loodiána are contemplating the establishment of a mission on this side the Sutlej. Shame to the Church of England, and particularly to those wealthy members of it among the laity at home and in this country, who ought to devote their riches to good purposes and to the service of God, instead of devoting them to the gratification of their own worldly pride and self-love!

4*th.—Sham Chowrassee*, 11 miles. The Governor-General had issued a proclamation that people from all parts of the country might come and hold a fair at Hoshiarpoor, bringing their merchandise there for that purpose free from duty; but they did not choose to take advantage of the proposal, and no fair was held. All this country is very fertile.

Ezek. ix. 2. " One man among them was clothed with linen, with a writer's inkhorn by his side." I have seen this. In the hills I more than once met men with an inkpot and pencase all in one, made of brass or other metal, fastened to their belt at one side.

5th.—Kurtapoor, 12½ miles. Sandy soil all the way, but every appearance of fertility. This is rather a large town. A Gooroo lives in it. I went to see his house. A large gateway leads into the enclosure; in which on one side is the tomb of some former Gooroo towering up several stories and terminating in a dome, a very picturesque object; on the other side is the Gooroo's habitation. I went up several flights of steps, passing one or two open apartments, and at the top was shown into a suite of rooms carpeted (one of them with red velvet) and decorated with chandeliers of glass suspended from the ceiling, with mirrors,

European chairs, English time-pieces up in a corner, a large musical box, glass doors, glass and talc inlay-work over the pillars and ceiling, and with pictures of all sizes covering the walls as thickly as possible, and the most tawdry things imaginable. Such rooms are called *sheesha-mahul*.(j)
The Gooroo is certainly not a very intellectual-looking man. He says the place, where he lives, is 10,000 years old. He wore an English gold watch, for which he said he gave R. 500.

This is one of the new stations; the 4th Regiment of Native Cavalry is here.

6th.—(Sunday.)—Divine Service as usual. Yesterday Mr. Newbolt, of the Commissariat Department, from Jullunder, called on me. I am told he is a religious man; I hope I shall be able to form this judgment of him myself. A real Christian in the Indian army is a light shining in a dark place. But alas! there is much self-righteousness and much self-deception in what is called the religious world.

(j) *i. e.*, a place all hung with glass.

§ 2. TRIAL AND CONVICTION OF RAJAH LOL SINGH, AND ARRANGEMENTS FOR THE GOVERNMENT OF THE PUNJAB.

7th.—Byrowál, on the river Beeas; a long march of 18 miles through heavy sand, and not much cultivation perceptible. We had to cross a deep *nuddee,*([k]) the water coming up to our horses' girths. It is full of quicksands and very dangerous to ford. Though the part for our crossing was marked off with bamboos, yet even in this one of the artillery ammunition carriages sunk, and 64 rounds of ammunition were lost; and the guns would have been lost too, had not the men instantly dismounted from their horses, which were frightened and restive, and pulled the guns out. On this side of the water also are some dangerous places. I saw 3 camels up to their necks in quagmires;

([k]) A stream.

the poor creatures were afterwards extricated, though with extreme difficulty. I believe it is always more difficult to help camels out of dangerous and painful positions, than other beasts, because of their excessive state of fright and helplessness.

A bridge of 50 boats has been constructed here across the Beeas. It is very cold now: thermometer just before sunrise 39°, at noon 62°.

10th.—The Beeas abounds with *cyprinus roe*, a species of carp, good for eating; also with a species of *silurus* about the size of a large trout, but very ugly, like a tadpole, and eaten by the natives only; also with tortoises and porpoises and alligators. Some officers the other day went out fishing and are said to have caught more than 1,900 fish.

There are a great many pea-fowl in the villages round about: it is a sacred bird, and its destruction is not allowed by the natives.

Information has arrived that Mr. Currie has executed his commission at Lahore and is expected

TRIAL AND CONVICTION OF RAJAH LOL SINGH. 137

back in a few days. Lol Singh, it appears, has been found guilty of having instigated Shaikh Imámoodeen to refuse to give up Cashmeer to Gooláb Singh according to the treaty, by which we agreed that Gooláb Singh should have that territory in consideration of his paying us 75 lakhs of rupees, (¹) it having been ceded to us by the Lahore Government. Lol Singh was tried in open *durbár* on the 3rd and 4th instant in a tent on the plain opposite the palace. He was defended by Dewán Deena Náth, but he said nothing in his own defence, when charged; and Shaikh Imámoodeen produced the very letters signed, which Lol Singh had privately written to him. His guilt being clearly proved, the Court of Inquiry, consisting of Major-General Littler, Lieutenant-Colonel Lawrence, Lieutenant-Colonel Goldie, Mr. Currie, and Mr. J. Lawrence, retired to Mr. Currie's tent, and the Sirdárs by invitation accompanied them. The decision of the Court was then communicated to the Sirdárs, that Lol

(¹) A lakh is 100,000.

Singh must be deposed, or the British Government could hold no correspondence with the Lahore Durbár; to which decision they assented. The rest of the Sirdárs were then requested to withdraw, and Lol Singh was left alone with the British officers, who had conducted the prosecution. He was informed that he must go to his own house, but that he would not be permitted to enter the palace. Mr. Edwardes, Assistant to Colonel Lawrence, was deputed to escort him and to make him aware that he was no longer *wuzeer*. Thus he was escorted, mounted on his elephant and surrounded by his own guard, through the city to his own house; where for the present he is kept under surveillance, till farther measures are taken with respect to his location. He will probably be sent down to Benáres or somewhere a great distance off, to remain there for his life. Shaikh Imámoodeen is set at liberty.

Some think that Gooláb Singh himself, who is a notorious knave and hates Lol Singh, has been at the bottom of the plot and has made a fool of

Lol Singh for the very purpose of getting rid of him. Who can dive into the depths of Oriental cunning and treachery? Several battles were fought between the troops of the Shaikh and those of Gooláb, and the Shaikh did not surrender till we sent forces to Gooláb's aid. Colonel Lawrence has since gone into the valley of Cashmeer, to ascertain that all is quiet; which is the case, inasmuch as the Cashmeeries themselves took no part in the insurrection. After the trial of the Rájah was over, some of the Sirdárs expressed their astonishment to Mr. Currie, that he should have taken all the trouble of trying the Rájah, when every one knew and he (Mr. Currie) best of all, that there was no ·question of his guilt. Such are the notions, which these wretched creatures entertain, of justice and open dealing. How surprised would they be at many cases of our trial by jury! It is to be hoped that we shall reform their notions upon many subjects in process of time. I am sure they must be astounded at our generous and lenient conduct towards Lol Singh and towards the Lahore Government after the discovery of this plot. Many treaties have been considered null and void by civilized powers on less justifiable grounds, than our treaty with Lahore might have been by us on the present occasion; and we have had an opportunity of taking possession of the Punjáb, of which we might have availed ourselves with less breach of faith, than has often been committed by Christian Governments. Our honourable and forbearing policy towards our conquered enemies must have a mighty moral effect upon the native mind throughout the whole of India. Such is one of the inestimable blessings attendant upon Christianity.

The Government of Lahore has been placed *pro tempore* in the hands of four, viz., Dewán Deena Náth, Sirdar Téj Singh, Sirdar Shér Singh, and Khaleefa Nooroodeen.

This morning at sunrise thermometer 36°.

I rejoiced to hear the other day from Mr. Currie, that our Government are about to issue an order prohibiting the prosecution of public works on Sundays.(*m*) The desecration ought never to have been allowed; but the correction is better late than never and does credit to Lord Hardinge's administration. In excuse for the employment of heathen labourers by Christian masters on Sunday it is constantly alleged, that the day is nothing to heathens, and that, as they do not respect it, they ought to be at liberty to work upon it. But is that a reason why the day should be nothing to their Christian masters and `employers? and is not the employment of labourers, whoever they may be, forbidden? Because the day is nothing to heathens, does it follow that they ought to be employed by Christian masters to work upon it? Did the Jews employ heathen labourers on their Sabbath? for we read that " their bondmen and bondmaids were of the heathen that were round about them ; of them

(*m*) But I grieve to say that the order above referred to has not been honoured with due observance : public works are still prosecuted on Sunday.

they bought bondmen and bondmaids." Levit. xxv. 44. Besides, if *the Lord's day* is nothing to heathens, still the *Sunday* should be something— for the name itself is heathen, and the day is a sacred day in the Hindoo religion; its Sanskrit name is *rabeebár*. But, if we wish Hindoos or other heathens to embrace Christianity, we shall certainly not induce them to do so by showing them our disregard for Divine Commandments, which we profess to obey.

11*th*.—The poor people on both sides of the river appear remarkably civil. There is no perceptible difference between the dirty mud villages and the squalid exterior and nudity of the natives here and those, with which we are familiar in Hindoostán. The countenances of the females are just as ugly; but I think there is greater wickedness in the faces of the men. There are many of the disbanded Seekh soldiers about, some working at the plough with their old red jackets on: they must find it a rather uncongenial occupation after the life they have been trained to.

ARRANGEMENTS FOR THE GOVERNMENT, ETC. 143

12*th*.—Chilblains on my feet; but no wonder: the thermometer every morning before sunrise is down at freezing point; and at night the sand, which is the ground here, is as cold as ice, and the *shutrunjee* (*) of a tent is not the least protection against it.

13*th*.—(Sunday.)—Divine Service as usual.

14*th*.—I understand that a British force will continue to occupy Lahore, but that the wretched subsidiary system, which is maintained in Oude and Gwálior, will not be established here; and certainly it is to be hoped not: for by this system all kinds of injustice and oppression practised by the native Government are countenanced and supported by British authority.

Yesterday evening I took a walk with Captain Harrison, and our conversation turned upon the Church in Ireland. I expressed my fear that the present Ministry would be proposing to endow the Church of Rome in that unhappy country. We discussed the subject of religious toleration, con-

(*) A kind of carpet.

nection of Church and State, &c. (to use the conventional, but incorrect phrases). My friend contended that liberty of conscience (another incorrect phrase) and religious toleration, as it is called, seemed almost to justify the endowment, and also that the same principles seemed opposed to the connection of Church and State. I maintained toleration, but not sanction and support; which two distinct and different things are generally confounded the one with the other. On the same ground I held that Hindooism and Muhummedanism ought not to be fostered and patronized, while the progress of Christianity was discouraged and unsupported, by the British Government. The plea of liberty of conscience might be urged for the endowment and sanction of almost everything wrong, not only hydra-headed dissent, which according to its own principles might and ought to multiply itself indefinitely, till every individual set up himself alone as a separate *sect* (°) and separate *denomination* (°), being himself the teacher

(°) The very terms are condemned in the Epistles of

and the taught, the ruler and the ruled in one, but even infidelity; and not only so, but immorality also; and not only so, but practices subversive of political order and inconsistent with submission to civil government—practices to which not even *toleration* could be extended. I maintained the expediency of the ecclesiastical system and externals of the Church of England being established and defended by the laws of the British State, and of its being recognised as the National Church, and its claim upon the State for temporal aid and support; also the duty of a Christian Government to help forward the propagation of the Gospel among heathen nations. But what, if the State betray the Church?

15*th.*—I saw some boys in a village playing at *ball* like English school-boys.

I have just been reading this—" A deaf and

St. Paul; and yet they are used now as indicative not of something to be ashamed of, not of an unchristian state of schism and faction, but of an innocent or even laudable state of advancement, freedom, and enlightenment, almost to be boasted of.

L

dumb boy, being asked what forgiveness was, took a pencil and wrote, 'It is the sweetness, which flowers give when trampled on.'" What a quantity of sweetness therefore ought to proceed from the poorer and humbler portion of our fallen race, whose worldly condition exposes them to the contumely and insolence, and ridicule and contemptuous bearing, and unjust and oppressive dealing of the rich and proud! and what a quantity of "stink and ill savour must come up" from the latter, who not only insult and wrong their poorer brethren, but make their own ill odour more offensive still by deeming it *infra dignitatem* to apologize, to say, "I repent," which is the divinely enjoined preliminary to forgiveness! (Luke xvii. 4.) Victims of insult and overbearing pride, rejoice: "for great is your reward in heaven:" for "the first shall be last and the last first;" and who are the chosen "heirs of the kingdom," but the "poor of this world, who are rich in faith?"

16*th*.—A species of crocodile called *ghureeyál* (a

Sanskrit name, but the only name it is known by) was caught in the river by a party fishing. It measured in length more than 15 feet and in greatest width 5 feet. It has been dissected by Dr. Walker (*q*); and we found the lungs full of small white pellucid worms; 11 ribs on each side; the stomach very large and full of half-digested fish and fishes' backbones and a quantity of stones, the largest of which I have in my possession, being about the size of a hen's egg, which stones it is supposed the animal swallows for the purpose of effecting the digestion of its food, like poultry; the windpipe curved in this form ; several lumps of conglomerated sand inside the chest, one in the throat; two bullets of lead, one in the pericardium, the other in the vicinity of the penis, which must have been there a long time, as they were grown over with membrane and fat; the intestines 23 feet in length; the testicles very large and inside the abdomen; excito-motory convulsion strong during dissection. The animal has

(*q*) Surgeon to the Governor-General.

an elongated snout about 2 feet in length, full of large teeth, with a protuberance of flesh at the end furnished with nostrils, which it raises above the water to inhale air: I have often seen it in this position in the Ganges, remaining so for a long time in the same spot near the edge of the river. This species of crocodile abounds in the Ganges and is harmless.

17*th.*—This evening I saw some village boys lustily playing at bandy; I never saw boys in Hindoostán playing at any game of the kind. No doubt these active sports have something to do with the fine athletic figures and constitutions of the natives here, just as in our own country.

18*th.*—Anniversary of the battle of Moodkee; no commemoration of the day. This evening Mr. Currie returned from Lahore. At present affairs have a more pacific aspect. Arrangements will be made for the supremacy of British authority at Lahore: our troops will remain there; our laws will be gradually introduced. The possession of the Punjáb is virtually ours, though the Máharájah is

ARRANGEMENTS FOR THE GOVERNMENT, ETC. 149

acknowledged and a nominal Seekh Government will be maintained. The Máharájah is to come here on a visit to the Governor-General next week, and the Governor-General will return it by going to Lahore.

20th.—(Sunday.)—Divine Service as usual. Last night we had a sharp shower with a loud clap of thunder; to-day the air is warmer than it was, but still delightfully cool.

21st.—Anniversary of the battle of Ferozeshahr. The Governor-General entertained a large party at dinner, and after dinner made an appropriate speech.

One part of the Governor-General's wise policy now is the formation of regiments out of the disbanded Khalsa troops, who otherwise might be devising mischief.

25th. — Divine Service for Christmas-day. Congregation smaller than usual—only between 20 and 30 besides the band-boys; yet there are now in the camp the Body-guard, the 73rd Regiment N. I., the 2nd European L. I., and a troop of Horse Artillery. The Commander-in-Chief attended our Service. He has come to be present at the durbár to-morrow, which is to be held for the ratification of a fresh treaty with the Lahore Government, the treaty having been made on the 16th inst. This treaty differs from the first only in the 15th article, which stipulated the withdrawal of our troops at the end of the year, whereas the engagement now is, that, as the Seekh Sirdars cannot form a Government themselves, we keep our troops (10,000) there till the Máharájah attains his majority, *i. e.*, for eight years; that the government then be handed over to him and our troops withdrawn; that Colonel Lawrence be Resident at Lahore and have supreme jurisdiction, while a Council of five Sirdárs under him shall conduct the different departments of administration; that our troops be paid by the Lahore Government 22 lakhs of rupees a year.

26*th*.—Máharájah Dhuleep Singh arrived at the Governor-General's durbár-tent at 10 o'clock A.M. The Máharájah signed the treaty. The Governor-

General, seated on his vice-royal throne, delivered an address explaining the object of the British Government to be the welfare of the Lahore kingdom. Among the Chiefs, who were present, was the famous Shaikh Imámoodeen. During the address, which was interpreted to them by Mr. Currie, the Chiefs appeared perfectly listless and apathetic; but I understand they are dissatisfied and disappointed, and that they repented immediately after they had given assent to the terms of this treaty, which had been proposed to them at Lahore as the only alternative, if we were not at once and altogether to abandon their country. The durbár closed, as usual, with a profusion of *nuzzurs* consisting of jewels, shawls, guns, &c., the only part of the ceremony that seemed to interest and animate the Sirdár-lóg. All parties on our side seem to agree in affirming the wisdom of this present arrangement, even those, who entertain adverse opinions about the Governor-General's original policy. Truly a proud position is now occupied by the British Government; and how humiliating is that now occupied by our late antagonists!

27*th.*—(Sunday.)—Divine Service. Lord and Lady Gough attended. They leave to-morrow. My sermon of Christmas-day gave offence to one of the congregation then present, because I spoke of infidelity (meaning a disbelief in the peculiar doctrines of the New Testament) as criminal, he himself being a sceptic. The same offence has been occasioned by these doctrines from the very first day of their promulgation. Nor is it in the power of the Ministers of Christ to make or to prove infidelity less criminal, than He Himself has made it: " he that believeth not, shall be damned;"(*r*) " he shall not see life, but the wrath of God abideth on him;" (*s*) " if the Gospel be hid, it is hid to them that are lost." (*t*)

28*th.*—*Jundiála*, 15 miles, *en route* to Lahore.

29*th.*—*Umritsir*, 13 miles. Streets and people as dirty, as when I saw them last year. I went to-day to see the holy tank and the shrine, where

(*r*) Mark xvi. 16.   (*s*) John iii. 36.   (*t*) 2 Cor. iv. 3.

the oldest and most precious copy of the *Grunth* is kept. But they would not allow me to enter the sacred enclosure without taking off my boots. (^u) The tank is not visible from the outside of the enclosure, this being surrounded by high buildings and only accessible at one corner. The enclosure and the tank are square, with a broad paved walk all round. The sides of the quadrangle are occupied with the houses of Gooroos and Rájahs. Many Akálees also live here in gloomy-looking holes like dungeons. Besides the iron instruments like quoits or horse-shoes stuck in their head-dress, (^v) these demoniacs carry also a short club to throw at the objects of their fury; such weapons corresponding, I suppose, in the quality they are charged with to the *brahm-ástur*. (^w) I saw several

---

(^u) I see no harm in my compliance. Rom. xiv. and 1 Cor. viii. do not apply to such a case. But some people "strain at a gnat and swallow a camel."

(^v) See above, p. 105.

(^w) A fabled weapon, which, after consecration by a formula addressed to Brahma, deals infallible destruction to those, against whom it is discharged.

of these wretched creatures about. Two years ago it would have been dangerous for a Faringee to be so near them. In the middle of the tank is the shrine, of white marble, square, two stories high, the exterior covered with gold, except in parts where it is inlaid. The *Grunth Sáhib* (so called by way of respect) is kept inside on the floor, covered with a cloth, so that no one can see it, and over the cloth is a canopy of red velvet. Behind it sits an aged Gooroo, with a *chowree* (*x*) to keep off the flies or anything whose contact might pollute the holy thing. In front of it is a heap of shells (*kowrees*), which are the votive offerings of the people to the sacred book. On each side of the old white-bearded Gooroo sit a number of other Gooroos, and on one side musicians playing on their drums and *sitárs*. (*y*) In front of all, crowding in at the doorway, are the people, who come to worship, the object of worship being the *Grunth*. The place swarms with people all day

(*x*) A large waving brush.
(*y*) A kind of guitar with three strings.

long, not only the inhabitants of Umritsir, but pilgrims from all parts of the country. The shrine is connected with one side of the tank by a handsome broad viaduct of white marble. I asked if I could see the book, but was not allowed. It is never uncovered, except early in the morning. The old Gooroo sent me by the hand of one of the dirty people present a sloppy piece of his sweetmeat to eat, as a great honor. He never leaves his place, they say, except at midnight: he has three fellow-labourers, who take the duty in turn with him. In another part of the quadrangle is a building with a gilt dome, which I believe is their senate-house. A fine view of the town is commanded from the top of some of the minárs. In walking round the square I passed by several *Grunths*, all covered up except one, some out of doors on the ground, others in small shrines. The whole was built in the reign of Runjeet Singh. In returning home my eye was caught by a disgustingly indecent figure in front of one of the houses.

I could not obtain admittance into the fort, Govindgurh, in consequence of some order that has been issued by the Governor-General. During our stay here two of our own sentries have been posted at the gate of the fort; a circumstance which deserves remark: as it seems to presage our actual possession of Govindgurh some day or other.

I hear that in the Jullunder Dooáb, since our possession of it, a lakh of rupees has reverted to the people in the form of immunity from taxes, which used to be levied by the Seekh government: the Seekhs used to tax almost every article that can be named—nearly as bad as Vespasian and not much worse than a great and illustrious State of modern times, for which however I have a most patriotic veneration.

30th.—*Bhopoora*, 10 miles.

31st.—*Kunchuniónka pull*(*z*) (bridge of dancing girls or harlots), 10 miles.

(*z*) Called simply *pull* in the former journal.

§ 3. THE CITY OF LAHORE.

JAN. 1*st*, 1847.—*Shálamáh*, 10 miles. The famous garden here was illuminated this evening, and the Governor-General's arrival again in this neighbourhood was celebrated with a display of fireworks. The rockets were good; the style of illumination was the same as that at Pinjore.

The beginning of another year. Praised be God. Why has He kept me in this world till now? To try me longer; to give me additional time and opportunities for more perfect obedience to his will and greater meetness for heaven. Alas! how little use have I made of his goodness! how little have I done in my Master's cause! Am I fit to depart and be with Christ? Am I fit to enter into the joy of my Lord? O my Lord, give me grace, that I may spend as much of this year, as Thou shalt be pleased to prolong my days upon earth, more faithfully to Thee and more profitably to the working out of my salvation and that of my brethren, for whom Thou hast committed unto me the ministry of Thy Word and commissioned me to hold the exalted office of a Presbyter of the Church and a Steward of thy mysteries; and pardon me for all my past negligences, deficiencies, and sins, through the precious blood shed for me.

2nd.—Lahore. Our camp is close to the walls of the palace. The troops were all drawn out in a line round the camp and inspected by Lord Hardinge in company with the Máharájah and the Ránee,(*a*) who was of course concealed from view in a palankeen.

3rd.—(Sunday.)—Divine service, as usual, in the Governor-General's tent. Thin congregation. Captain Say, 45th N.I., a religious man, whose acquaintance I had made at Simla, spent the day with me. After service General Littler called on me. In the evening Captain Say and I walked

(*a*) The queen, who was a most abandoned character.

THE CITY OF LAHORE. 159

round the walls of the city, about three miles and a half in circuit, and met with five drunken Europeans in succession; two of whom I conducted home with the aid of two seepáhees, whom we procured from the officer in charge of one of the city-gates, fearing lest, if they remained all night in the place where they were, they might be murdered and stripped. What a shocking exhibition of our religious and moral character to the Seekhs! The stuff these wretched countrymen of ours drink is the same vile spirit, with which the Seekhs intoxicate themselves.

I am glad to find that Divine Service is held here every Sunday: the morning prayer of our Liturgy is offered in the open air, and Brigadier Eckford leads the devotions. This at least must show the Seekhs that we *have* a professed religion. I wish some able missionary were here to tell them more about it. I am pleased to hear from Brigadier Eckford, that on the whole the European soldiers have been orderly and sober.

4*th.*—The inhabitants of the city appear as

quiet and civil, as if we had ruled them for a hundred years. Dyce Anund, so called because a Mr. Dyce was his godfather, son of Anund Mussee, paid me a visit to-day; he is appointed adjutant in one of the Seekh regiments here. He tells me that he has in his possession a Véd two hundred years old; in which mention is made of the Messiah as being Lord of all things in heaven and earth.(*b*) I called on General Littler, Colonel Lawrence, and Brigadier Eckford, each of whom has comfortable quarters in the city.

5th.—I visited the tomb of king Jehángeer across the river, the ancient Hydraotes, now called Rávee. Like all other royal Mohummedan tombs, it is very handsome. I was struck with surprise at not being asked to take off my boots; I inquired the reason, and the men in charge replied, that, because the Sáhib lóg would not take

(*b*) He afterwards sent me a copy of the passage he referred to, taken from the 4th chapter of the Reeg Véd, in which the word *Musih* occurs; but I have not seen the original; besides, in the copied passage I can see nothing necessarily beyond a mere verbal or syllabic coincidence.

off their boots, therefore they had given up asking them. The tomb is in a dilapidated state, and no one cares about its repair. I also visited Runjeet Singh's tomb, which is within the walls of the city under the palace; it is superbly adorned with gold, &c. What a contrast to the simple *tumulus* of the Christian cottager in a village-churchyard at home!

I dined this evening with Colonel Lawrence, who is living in Soochet Singh's house. The houses of the Seekhs are built with strong thick walls, an open court in the middle, and three or four stories high; the apartments are small, the offices on the ground floor, and the rooms for the family above; the houses are very hot in summer.

6th.—Moulvee Tájdeen, nephew of Khaleefa Nooroodeen, and son of Imámoodeen, called with Dyce Anund on me to-day, to ask me a few questions about our religion. He inquired, what was the great commandment of our law; what was the difference between Roman Catholic and Protestant (alas! that such differences should exist and form a stumbling-block to the heathen); in what language the Scriptures were originally written; and when Christ will come again, as he had heard it was the opinion and announcement of Dr. Joseph Wolff, who visited Lahore in Runjeet Singh's time, that Christ would return in 1845. He said that he could not understand the justice of an innocent person dying for the guilty; but I told him that it was the infinite love of God towards His fallen creatures, upon which he seemed to have less difficulty in understanding the justice. He appears anxious to prosecute his inquiries. He has a copy of Martyn's Oordoo New Testament; so I gave him a Prayer-book in Oordoo and some tracts, which he seemed glad to accept. When he shook hands with me at parting, he had a gold coin in his hand, which he meant, according to custom, to offer me as a *nuzzur*, but which I left where it was. His father built the fort, Govindgurh, about forty years ago. The Seekhs generally are not disposed to learn what our religion is, and they have no doubts or misgivings about their own.

There are no Jews in Lahore; one lived here some years ago, a merchant; but, as far as I can learn, not one of that scattered and most interesting people, still "beloved for the fathers' sakes," is residing here at present.

The Máharájah held a durbár to-day for the Governor-General in the beautiful hall of audience. The two hours were occupied with conversation of no importance and the presentation of nuzzurs. Dhuleep Singh is a sharp intelligent-looking boy.

Before I went in, on dismounting I left in my sáees's (*c*) charge a Prayer-book, which I had occasion to use, and a pistol, which I had just bought as a curiosity, (strange companions certainly); when I came out and perceived they were missing, I asked him what had become of them, and he told me, with the most innocent surprise at my question, that during my absence somebody had come to him with a message from me that I wanted

(*c*) Groom's.

them immediately — a trick, which I consider quite worthy of a first-rate London sharper.

7th.—The Governor-General had a large dinner-party. After dinner came in by invitation Sirdárs Téj Singh and Shér Singh and the rest of the Council of Agency; they sat round on each side of the Governor-General at a little distance from the table; while his Lordship gave some toasts, one of which was the health of the Máharájah, another that of Téj Singh and his compeers, the toasts being drunk with enthusiastic hurrahs, which the honoured guests would not perhaps at the time understand, but which would no doubt be explained to them. Several of them were murderers, and, I dare say, would have no objection, if occasion served, to cut our throats.

Colonel Cortlandt, commanding a Seekh battalion, called on me to-day. He informed me that he had seen a spot on the other side of the Jhelum (ancient Hydaspes), where is a large conical building of stone, supposed to have been erected by Alexander the Great; that there are no steps for ascending it; that at the top is a cistern for water, and at the bottom was discovered by General Ventura, who had an excavation made from the top, a large solid stone enclosing three chests or boxes, one of copper, round which were stuck copper coins, another of silver inside it with silver coins, and inside that again another of gold containing gold coins; and that the neighbourhood abounds with coins, but on this side of the Jhelum none are found. He says that numbers of coins are hawked about the country, being chiefly those of Menander's reign, but that many are counterfeit. He describes the people of Káfiristán (or land of infidels, as the Mohummedans call them, with whom the Mohummedans are continually waging war,) as being a fine athletic race and exhibiting strongly marked traces of Grecian origin; though at the same time he says they have Roman noses.

8*th*.—I went this morning to Colonel Cortlandt's house in the cantonments at Meeanmeer to breakfast and to baptize his child. One of the sponsors was Colonel Steinbach, formerly in the Seekh service. As a mark of gratitude, which I am sure from their manner towards me and their reverential demeanour during the baptismal service they deeply felt, Colonel and Mrs. Cortlandt presented me with a handsome *chuga*([d]) of green silk embroidered with gold, such as is worn by the Sirdárs.

I dined at General Littler's and sat next to an officer, who thinks that the Jews will soon be restored to their country *as* Jews and will be a great political Power and assist in destroying the Church of Rome and the Mohummedan delusion, and that they are the Ancient of days and also the Stone, which should break the image to pieces, mentioned by Daniel the prophet. What constant proof we have, that it is far wiser for men and women " not to exercise themselves in great matters and in things too high for them!" (Ps. 131.) What excellent advice is given by the author of " The imitation of Christ!" " Never read the Word of God in order to appear more learned or

([d]) A cloak with sleeves.

more wise. Be studious for the mortification of thy sins: for this will profit thee more, than the knowledge of many difficult questions." "A man profits more by loving God and forsaking all things, than in studying subtleties." (B. iv. ch. 43.)

The dogs here are an intolerable nuisance and infest every part of the neighbourhood: one cannot take a ride without being tormented by a pack of them. Máharájah Runjeet Singh used to pay for their being fed, and the custom of feeding them remains to this day, but the pay, I imagine, is discontinued. The natives have a superstitious reverence for these brutes and never destroy them. The same feeling prevails in Hindoostan, and a regard for brute life connected with a belief in metempsychosis. How strangely inconsistent with the too common disregard for human life!

On my return home I found on my table a note recommending that, as I did not appear at the Máharájah's durbár on the 6th inst. and my present on that occasion would have been a pearl necklace and a pair of gold bangles, I should attend at the palace to-morrow for the purpose of being invested with my insignia; as if it were likely I should go—how ridiculous! and the note is written by a native Christian—kindly meant, but how childish!

9*th*.—The Governor-General held a durbár for the reception of the Máharájah.

10*th*.—(Sunday.)—Divine service, as usual. Many of the soldiers in hospital here are suffering from sore eyes. This complaint is not uncommon among our soldiers in India. It is said that some of them purposely injure their own eyes, to escape from service and return to England; and that the diagnostics of surgical science cannot always detect the trickery; but I think such cases must be rare.(*e*) I have given New Testaments and

---

(*e*) I understand that now soldiers, who become blind in India from ophthalmia, are not allowed to return to Europe: the object being to deter men from the imposture above-mentioned. But this regulation falls heavy and hard upon the innocent.

tracts to several of the sick men, who have been glad to receive them. I do not know how it is: every soldier ought to have his Bible and Prayer-book; but I very rarely find in hospitals more than one or two, and when I ask where their Bibles are, the usual answer is either, "I have lost it," or "It is locked up in my box." A Roman Catholic priest has arrived at Lahore and visits the hospitals. No chaplain of our church has been sent here yet; but I believe one is to be appointed to this important sphere of labour. Brigadier Eckford talks to the men in hospital about "the things which belong to their everlasting peace;" he accompanied me there this afternoon. We are thankful for the co-operation of pious laymen, so long as they are not self-constituted helpers and keep within the bounds of their proper sphere. Modesty in things spiritual is a Christian grace and ornament sometimes not so conspicuous in lay members of the Church as it ought to be.

Many of our doings have astonished the natives,

and not least of all, our taking the trouble to clean their streets for them. Since our occupation of Lahore, the streets are quite clean, compared with what they were before. They must think the Farunghees a strange set of people.

We are to leave Lahore to-morrow; and I think we may leave it this time with the following reflections: that the wise policy of the British Government in the last treaty has a threefold evidence: 1st. The fact, that the continuance of our military occupation of the city and our superintendence of the administration of the country were *solicited* by the Lahore Durbár; 2nd. The daily diminution of their power and resources for mischief by the annual payment to us of 22 lakhs of rupees from the Lahore Government; 3rd. The preparation for avoidance of bloodshed and for greater facility in effecting, should circumstances hereafter compel us to effect, our final possession of the country; in which case, as natural philosophers used to say that "*compositio est opus hominum, mixtio opus naturæ*," so the present policy of our Government would be well calculated to produce the latter out of the former, or a perfect union and amalgamation out of an imperfect: moreover that the humanizing and correcting influences of Christian civilization will be introduced, and thus infanticide and other enormities, now held lawful, will in time be made criminal and abolished by the gradual adoption of our laws, as they are indeed already condemned by the dictates of common humanity and by every human conscience, unless or until distorted and hardened by vicious training and vicious practice: also that a way is now effectually opened for that most important and primary work of all, the communication of the awakening, alarming, and inviting messages of the Christian revelation.

§ 4. DEPARTURE FROM LAHORE AND PROSECUTION OF THE TOUR TO THE FOOT OF THE HILLS.

11th.—*Dahooree*, 12 miles; but Colonel Benson, Dr. Walker and myself, missed the road and made the distance about 18 miles.

12*th.*—*Beránee*, 11 miles.

13*th.*—*Bhynee*, 13½ miles. Our three last marches have been almost entirely through jungul. The scantiness of culture is owing no doubt to the thinness of the population. Much of Hindoostan is unproductive from the same cause. If peace continue here under our rule, the population will increase and this fertile soil be turned to good account. But "where Ottoman's horse sets his foot, people will come up very thin."

14*th.*—*Putteh*, 8 miles. Very poor cultivation. This is a Mohummedan town and the people say there is not one Seekh in it.

DEPARTURE FROM LAHORE, ETC. 173

15th.—Hurreeka puttun, 10 miles. *Puttun* is probably *i. q. pultun,* regiment, which is not an Oriental word, but a corruption of *battalion.* *Hurree* is supposed to be *i. q.* Hercules, from whom therefore this place is said to have derived its name; (′) but it is a Sanskrit word and a name of Vishnoo, and so, if Hindoo mythology be partly derived from Greece, the identity between Hercules and Vishnoo would seem obvious, and not that between Jesus and Vishnoo, as if these might be the same word in different forms. Here is the ford, where Rájah Lol Singh with part of the Seekh force crossed before the battle of Ferozeshuhr; the rest crossed at Atáreewolla lower down; and here they all crossed after the battle.

16th.—Bootawoolla, 6 miles down the river. This place is about two miles from Sobráon, where the battle was fought, or two miles from the river;

(′) Major James Abbott says, " The name Hericulea is still borne by women in Bengal." On the sites of Nikaia and Boukephalon.—Journal of the Asiatic Society of Bengal, No. iii., 1852, p. 249.

for the river was close in the rear of the Seekh trenches. A considerable part of the entrenchments still remains, though a large portion of the field of battle has been swept away by the encroachments of the river. A great part of the wall has been knocked or worn down and is not now half the height it was; and a great part of the ditches has been filled up, perhaps with dead bodies, perhaps with alluvion from the ruins. I saw a pile of stones at one point of the battery, to mark the place where General Dick's division attacked and where he fell. Rhodawolla is between Bootawolla and Sobráon. All the villages here are Mohummedan and so much alike, that it is difficult to find one's road in the distant open plain covered with low jungul.

17th.—(Sunday.)—Divine service as usual.

19th.—*Ahmedwolla*, 8½ miles. Desert plain.

20th.—*Ferozeshuhr*, 8 miles. Bushy jungul all the way. Traces of the great battle are still perceptible in skulls and bones and rags and fragments of red jackets strewed about the plain. I could discover no remains of the trenches, though some, who were in the engagement, say they might be traced. In one spot is a cluster of graves, where some of our countrymen must have been buried. A quantity of dried skin, like leather, lies scattered about, which I am assured by the natives is human skin parched and hardened by the sun. I found one skull partly covered with skin and hair, the skin being in the state just described. I was amused at some of our seepáhees, who were looking at one of the skulls and showed it to me as something very wonderful: for, pointing out the serrated sutures, they declared that it was writing, and, though not legible to them nor to me, whom they asked to interpret the writing, God had engraved it there at his first formation to mark the man's destiny in letters on his skull.

21*st.—Moodkee*, 8 miles. Between two and three miles from Moodkee is the village of Lohám, where the battle ended, being about a mile and a half from where it began, *i. e.* from the entrance into the thick high bush-jungul, which covers most of the intervening ground: so that last year's accounts were exaggerated, which stated that we pursued the enemy four or five miles. But what a place for a field of battle! I see no remains on the ground except bones of beasts. Our camp is pitched on nearly the same spot, which it occupied last year. A cluster of little mounds close by marks the burial place of some of our brave brethren.

22nd.—Bhága purána, 16 miles. We came by the same heavy sandy road last year with the army; I remember it perfectly, and especially one or two spots associated in my mind with particular incidents; one is the spot, where we received a false report of the approach of the enemy and the troops were ordered to form into line and the artillery to unlimber; though the same evening proved that the enemy were not very far off. The weather is unusually warm for this season of the year.

23rd.—Wudnee, 12 miles. Unpleasant recollection of the appearance of the fort last year. The Governor-General was pleased to thank me for my sermon of last Sunday: I firmly believe it was nothing but the truth.

24th.—(Sunday.)—Divine Service as usual. A rainy day. Colonel Abbott of the Engineers appears to be a religious man without palaver and parade.

25th.—*Bussean*, 16 miles. Fine cultivation of wheat, gram, and mustard. Cold wind all day, and heavy rain in the evening.

26th.—*Lohát-buddea*, 10 miles. Rain prevented our marching before breakfast; so we marched after, but part of the camp remained behind to come on to-morrow. We did not however escape from the contributions of the clouds, and all day with very little interval the contents of " the bottles of heaven" have been pouring down. The ground is one complete puddle. No shelter for the poor horses, and not an inch of dry bed for them at night; mine however together with my servants were accommodated during part of the day in the verandahs of my tent. On such days as this the native servants and camp-followers cannot bake their *chapátees* or cook anything out of doors, and so most of them get nothing to eat. But fasting is much easier to Oriental stomachs, than it is to ours. My own dinner to-day was cooked in the verandah of my tent, which of course was filled with smoke; but I thought it better to be half-blinded than half-famished.

27th.—Incessant rain last night, and the ground of the verandahs, where the servants slept, almost as wet as out of doors. Fourteen natives of our camp, besides cattle, have died from exposure to the wet and cold. The wonder is, how any poor wretches, that live on *chapátees* and water and have no covering, but what is barely sufficient for decency, could survive such exposure after a whole day's fasting.

28th.—Anniversary of Alleewál. Fine weather. We have been halting, to allow time for the tents at the former encamping ground to dry and be brought on.

29*th.—Mullair kotla,* 14¼ miles. This is a large walled town; a Nawáb lives here, whose name is Soobah Khán, son of Ameer Khán, and he came out to meet the Governor-General. I understand this Nawáb took part against us in the late war. In all this country, that we are passing through, the cultivation is very rich. The farmers understand well how to protect their fields with hedges: the material being a sort of dead bramble, not indeed to be compared with our quick-set hedges in England, but still quite sufficient to keep out any cattle, &c. The camp-followers, though strictly watched and punished, when caught plundering, steal this hedge-wood to burn, and the sound produced is certainly a "crackling of thorns." The natives delight in a great blaze; they all stand round it in a ring, and when the blaze has subsided, they sit round the ashes, as long as a spark remains, and smoke their hookkas, chattering about *pysa* and *khána,* the all-absorbing and almost the only topics of conversation with them. The other day some villanous camp-followers stole a quantity of this hedge-wood and made the poor *raiyuts*, to whom it belonged, carry it for them to the camp, beating them along the road with their sticks and clubs, which they pretend to keep for self-defence. To-day and yesterday the air has been more English, than I ever remember feeling it in India; and the wind has been cold and bracing.

30*th.*—*Oomergurh*, 10 miles. Sharp wind.

31*st.*—(Sunday.)—*Nábah*, 12 miles. The reason I have heard assigned for marching to-day is, that his Lordship thought it better to leave the wet ground, where we were encamped yesterday. Divine Service was held as usual; but of course few were able to attend. I am sorry to hear that office work is constantly done in camp on Sundays: no doubt it is sometimes necessary; but the natives do not understand the consistency of such practice with our professed religion. How different however is the observance of Sunday now in India from what it was, or rather was not, in former days, before any chaplains or churches existed in the country, when the natives, at a loss to conceive what our religion could be, and perceiving no better signs of it, concluded that the pacing of the Sáhibs up and down the verandahs of their *bunglás* must be their *pooja*.(*q*) A Rájah resides here; he came out to meet the Governor-General. I believe that this potentate also took part against us in the late war.

February 1*st.*—*Dublán*, 8 miles. A very pretty road. A cold misty day; thermometer at noon in tent 53°. Mohun Lol, who calls himself *Esquire,* and who has been absurdly made so much of in England, is here in a tent of his own; but what his business here is I know not; they say that he wants some political employment. He is a heathen. I wish our Government would employ more native Christians in their service; the plea against their employment is that State-patronage might encourage hypocrisy; but is evil to be done, that good may come? and is it not evil, to reject a fellow-creature and refuse him the means of

(*q*) Worship.

livelihood simply because he is a fellow-Christian? Is this the spirit of our holy religion? Jesus said, "Except a man forsake father and mother, brethren and sisters, houses and lands, for my sake, he cannot be my disciple;" but did He authorize the Church, did He authorize those who were already converted to the Faith, did He authorize a Christian Government, to increase the hardship and to throw additional obstacles in the way of the conversion of others? to discourage and turn our backs upon our fellow-creatures, who have already submitted to the sacrifice and self-denial He requires as a test of sincerity, and who have come into His fold with the hope and reasonable expectation of finding sympathy, support, and comfort? Hypocrites there may be and martyrs there will be; but it is no business of ours to anticipate and prejudge hypocrisy or to make the martyr by persecution: better to judge ourselves by the test prescribed for *us*, and to make the sacrifices demanded from us in proof of *our own* sincerity.

2nd.—*Puttiála*, 9 miles. This is a large town, almost as filthy as Lahore was before we cleaned it. The Rájah came out to meet the Governor-General. I understand that this Rájah has an army of several thousand men and 20 guns. I have heard it remarked of this town, that no women are ever seen in it; but my own observation does not confirm this remark: the streets, that I went through, were graced with their share of the *fair* sex, though uglier daughters of Eve I never beheld.

3rd.—Yesterday the ground was deluged with rain; to-day it is fine, but very cold. His Lordship held a durbár for the Rájah.

4th.—The same honour was done to-day to his Lordship by the Rájah, whose palace is in the middle of the town, a fine building, four stories high, the front reminding me of the *aubérges* in Valetta. The durbár-room was not so handsome as that at Lahore; it was adorned with European mirrors and chandeliers and hall-lamps, some of plain, others of stained glass, with things called pictures, and with a crimson-velvet carpet. During the durbár a group of nátch(*h*)-girls danced and sang, or rather screeched, in front of us—a diversion, to which we would rather not have been doomed: the singing and music were execrable, though all alike was meant, and therefore to be appreciated, as part of the hospitality and honour. Another pastime was tying a horse up in a blanket; but this was nothing wonderful, as his head was left out. At dusk the palace-yard was all in a blaze with fireworks and various pyrotechnic manœuvres. Among the *nuzzurs* was a cloak lined with sable and also a bow of steel, not of silver, though still recalling to mind old Homer's description—

$$\delta\epsilon\iota\nu\grave{\eta} \ \delta\grave{\epsilon} \ \kappa\lambda\alpha\gamma\gamma\grave{\eta} \ '\gamma\acute{\iota}\nu\epsilon\tau' \ \mathring{a}\rho\gamma\upsilon\rho\acute{\epsilon}o\iota o \ \beta\acute{\iota}o\iota o.$$

5th.—Some pretty rides in this neighbourhood. I went this evening to Bahádur gurh, a new fort about 5 miles off, built by Kurrum Singh, father of the present Rájah, and apparently constructed

(*h*) Dance.

as much for ornament and for a royal residence, as
for any other purpose. The Governor-General
went to see it, preceded by the Máharájah. I was
too late and arrived just as they were coming
away; but the Máharájah most courteously
ordered that I might be shown over the palace.
It is worth seeing, because such a building of
recent date is a rare spectacle in India: the native
sovereigns do not build now, as they did in times
antecedent to the British rule. I understand that
in this fort there is one point of perfection, viz.,
that the glacis is level with the top of the enclosed
building, so that no object within is visible to an
enemy without. An annual tribute in the form of
transit duties to the amount of Rs. 50,000 has been
exacted from the Rájah by our Government, in
consideration of which he receives two guns, so
that his ordnance will consist of 22 pieces, and
also a handsome dressing-case, which belonged to
Napoleon, besides other valuable presents. I am
informed that the moral character of this Rájah
is better than that of native princes in general.

6th.—*Korálee,* 12 miles. Very pretty road. Weather now delightful.

7th.—(Sunday.)—Divine Service, as usual. I have received a distressing letter from my native Christian friend at Bishop's College. Oh that all our converts had a spirit of indifference and contempt for mere outward distinctions, and at the same time that a better example were set them in this respect by my countrymen, and also that due consideration were had for their remaining prejudices in accordance with the apostle's instructions for the treatment of weak consciences!

8th.—Rain fell all last night and obliges us to halt another day.

9th.—*Bhoona,* 12 miles. Road nothing but mud.

10th.—*Khytul,* 14 miles. First half of the road mud, the other half as good as any English turnpike-road. This is a large town with a fort, which is a pretty object, containing a palace built by the late Rájah some thirty years ago. The palace is four stories high and commands an extensive view; in front are winged human figures in stone like those which we make to represent angels. Outside the fort is another royal residence, but smaller, built by the same Rájah about twelve years ago; on the ground-floor of which are two very large handsome rooms, the most handsome I have seen in India, the roof of one of them being supported by four massive Corinthian pillars. On the death of the late Rájah, Khytul reverted to the British according to treaty; but the Ránee was rebellious and refused to surrender it; whereupon our Government sent a force to compel her submission. This occurred in the time of Lord Ellenborough. Monkeys abound here; and here also is a sacred tank for bathing, the water of which is said by the natives to come from the holy river Sasoota; this river we crossed on our road: it is the famous stream, which the native fable reports to disappear somewhere in this neighbourhood and after a subterranean course to make its exit again at Allahabád.

11*th.—Futtehpore*, 12 miles. Excellent road. The country here is very inviting to sportsmen:

it abounds with hares, partridges, teal, wild geese, and, I am told, wild boars also.

12*th.*—*Neesing*, 13 miles. Excellent road.

13*th.*—*Kurnál*, 15 miles. The same as it was last year in appearance, except that the bunglas have gone through another stage of dilapidation. A civilian is residing here, but no other European. I went into the church again: what a melancholy sight, so fine a church deserted by the Spirit of God and the voice of His ministers, and only awaiting the quick ravages of time to fall to ruin! The general impression is, that if proper drainage and purification had been resorted to, this large station need not have been condemned and deserted.

14*th.*—(Sunday.)—Divine Service, as usual. A very wet day and very small congregation.

16*th.*—A beautiful drive, planted with trees on each side, extends about two miles and a half along the border of the canal; and it is now overgrown with turf, which adds to its beauty. The canal is called the Dehli canal and was constructed by Feroze Sháh or King Feroze.

DEPARTURE FROM LAHORE, ETC. 189

17th.—Bedowlee, 12 miles. We crossed the Jumna by a bridge of twenty boats. I have been living for the last week on hares and partridges, daily presents from my young sporting neighbours; but they are very insipid, compared with English game.

18th.—Shámlee, 15 miles. Our encamping ground to-day is in a grove of mango-trees. We are close to the Dooáb canal, a work of the British Government.

19th.—Korowah, 12 miles.

20th.—Nowgawa Ghát, 12 miles. A small stream here called Hindun. Weather much warmer.

21st.—(Sunday.)—Divine service. How painful to a minister to observe those near him sitting cross-legged during the prayers! Can a member of the Church of England justify such a posture? Can he conscientiously put himself by choice into such a posture for the purpose of supplication to the Almighty? Is it the attitude prescribed in the Prayer-book? Some people affect to maintain that postures are nothing; then why not have couches in church to lounge upon? but both natural and revealed religion teach a different doctrine; and Jesus Himself set a different example, and so did the apostles.

22nd. — *Sirdhána*, 8 miles. The palace of Bégum Sumroo is here. She was queen of this district, and built the palace with the assistance of European architects. It is built in the European fashion and furnished with English furniture; the walls of the rooms being hung with pictures of British officers, very well executed by a native artist of Meerut; only two pictures in her house came from England, one being a portrait of herself, the other of Sir David Ochterlony, for which latter she paid 1,000*l*. In the portrait of herself she is dressed as an English old lady. She was married to General Sombre, and became a member of the Church of Rome, though I do not learn who baptized her. Her income was about 12 lakhs of rupees. She lived *à la mode occidentale*. One apartment is a large ball-room, where she used to give splendid entertainments; in another is a billiard-table. All the rooms are on the same floor, but it is raised high above the ground and approached by a broad flight of steps and a fine verandah. At the top of the building is a terrace, reached by a winding staircase and commanding an extensive view. Attached to the house is a large garden, now in disorder, which in her lifetime was dressed by eighty gardeners. The spot was pointed out to us in her dining-room, where just under her chair she had one of her servant-girls, whose only crime was her beauty, buried alive with her head above the floor; the object of this method of interment being, that her heart might be delighted as often and as long as possible with the screams and groans of the perishing victim of her jealousy.[1]

Here also is a showy Roman Catholic Church, which the Bégum built in the year 1822, " *sub*

---

[1] The Bishop of Calcutta has a portrait of this monster in his palace. Surely, if it must be there, it were better for decency's sake to turn the face to the wall.

nomine et protectione Mariæ beatæ virginis," with two spires at the east end, a dome in the centre and two smaller domes at the west end. Three priests always reside here. They keep a boys' school, the number of boys being about forty, officers' sons I am told, perhaps non-commissioned officers, as the children are apparently half-castes. They have no native converts here, except one of the church-servants. Six servants take care of the church, and the *chuprass*(*k*) of each bears the figure of a cross. The only congregation therefore are the school-boys and the native officer in charge of the palace, Captain Swarry, a Roman Catholic from Gwálior. The school-house and the priests' house are all under one roof, and the edifice is called St. John's College.

23rd.—Meerut, 10 miles. I spent the day with Mr. Maddock, one of the chaplains of the station.

24th.—This evening at dinner at the Governor-General's table I sat opposite a Colonel in the Company's service, a notorious character, who was

(*k*) A brass plate worn on a belt.

talking about the seepáhees lately recovered from Affghanistan, where they had been taken captives or had settled themselves during the Affghan war; and he pronounced it as his opinion, that they should be restored to their caste, which they had lost, for that he believed caste to be the stronghold of British dominion in India, and therefore deserving in every way to be encouraged and maintained.

25th. — I spent part of each day with Mr. Maddock, whom I had the pleasure of knowing at Cánpoor. He and the senior chaplain, Mr. Hammond, are labouring hard together for the good of the people. The church has galleries, and is one of the largest in the country. There is no station in the Upper Provinces that I should prefer to this. Bunglas, gardens, roads, are all good, and there is abundance of riding ground. Mr. Maddock has established a native school on Christian principles, and the schoolmaster is a German, who can speak a little English, and is anxious to qualify himself for ordination; but he

o

expects a missionary from England shortly, to be sent out by the Church Missionary Society.

Two Roman Catholic priests live here, and they have a chapel with a congregation of 500 or 600. They do nothing as missionaries among the natives.

Sir F. Currie leaves us here, and goes to Calcutta to take his seat in Council. Mr. Elliott,([)]) late Secretary of the Revenue Department at Agra, succeeds him; he is said to be a clever man and an elegant scholar, which I am very glad to hear.

26*th.*—I have seen Matthew Prabhu Din, the

([)]) Afterwards Sir Henry Elliott. He died at the Cape of Good Hope, and has left behind him a reputation for talent, scholarship, and industry, which places his name among the brightest ornaments of the Civil Service of India, even though the laborious work, in which he was engaged, has been left incomplete, and his career as an author and a servant of the State cut so short by an overruling destiny—a reputation, which I venture to say, will not be acquired by many of those, whom the Universities of Oxford and Cambridge, and the new system of examination, will now prepare for the Honourable East India Company.

old Náyek, baptized by Mr. Fisher, the chaplain, in the year 1819. He says that Mr. Fisher did not understand the native language, and conversed with him through a Mohummedan coachman, who knew something of English. He also says that he was a Roman Catholic before, and was therefore not a convert from Hindooism; that he only conversed ten days with Mr. Fisher, and had not read much of the New Testament, and scarcely any of the Old, before his baptism; since which time, however, he has studied the Scriptures.

What necessity exists for giving our English names, themselves Anglicised from Greek or Latin, to natives of Hindoostán at their baptism? Some native converts, I believe, wish to adopt them, but not all; and why should the Hindoo nomenclature not suit as well as the Hindoo costume? It is objected to the retention of some of the Hindoo names, that they are the names of heathen deities, or derived from them; but this was not deemed in Apostolic days a hindrance to the retention of such names. Hermes, Dionysius, Apollos, Hymeneus, Epaphroditus, Nereus, did not drop their names on conversion to the Christian faith.

27*th.—Dowralla*, 8 miles. Very warm all day.

28*th.*—(Sunday).—Divine Service, as usual.

March 1*st.—Kuttowlee*, 12 miles. Fine crops. I am grieved at hearing, that it has been the custom of the Governors-General of India during their tours to give presents, consisting of large sums of Government money, to heathen temples and shrines, or to the priests in charge of them; but I hope the report may not be true.

2*nd.—Mozuffernuggur*, 12 miles. Yesterday and to-day the abominable Hindoo festival, called *Holee*, (what an incongruous name it sounds to an English ear!) has been celebrated; during which it is the privilege of Hindoos of both sexes to give utterance to all possible licentious language and obscene abuse of each other. " Out of the abundance of the heart the mouth speaketh," was said by One, who knew what was in man, and never boasted of the uprightness and purity of unregenerate human nature.

3rd.—*Kázeekepoor*, 15½ miles. We halt here two days for tiger-shooting—the tiger-jungul beginning here. A party of six went out, but found the ground of the jungul so swampy, that they were obliged to return. They saw the carcase of an ox half-devoured, but no tiger. Two wild boars were their only victims. One poor elephant sunk nearly up to the howdah in a bog; I believe it was extricated.

The new canal, called the Great Ganges Canal, will pass by this place. The work was begun by Lord Auckland, and stopped by Lord Ellenborough. The object for which it is designed is the irrigation of the country, and thereby an increase in the produce of the soil. The expectation is, that, when completed, it will pay Government 15 per cent. It is to be completed in 10 years. Twenty lákhs of rupees was the cost of it originally estimated, but the actual cost will far exceed that sum. The width is 140 feet, the depth 18 feet.

It will not be lined with masonry. Some people think it will not answer the purpose for which it is intended: time will show; but there are always adverse opinions about the utility of every enterprise. In point of magnitude this and the forthcoming (though, I fear, not *paulo post* future) railroad, or railroads, will, probably, be our chief public works in India, that our present generation will live to see.

On inquiring how it is that the natives will not discontinue that disgusting habit of eructation, which they are perpetually practising, not only in each other's faces, but in the presence of Sáhibs, I was amazed to learn, that they consider it a mark of politeness, and that among natives of all classes no greater compliment can be paid by a guest at his host's table, than to emit that abominable sound from the mouth in as deep and audible a tone as possible after the meal, in token that he has enjoyed a good and savoury dinner.

5*th.—Landowrah*, 12 miles. About 4 miles distant is the village of *Roorkee* or *Loorkee*, where a gigantic aqueduct for the Ganges Canal is being constructed across the bed of a torrent; it will be about half a mile long and 70 feet wide, and the foundation is 30 feet deep; it has been in progress one year, and will be finished in two years more.

The country we have been lately passing through is thickly studded with *sutteewárs*,(*m*) black with the smoke of many a human sacrifice. I trust they are now disused; though one of those I saw to-day appeared quite new, as if recently built for use. The *sutteewár* is a small square or oblong structure of stone or brick, with 4 pillars at the corners, and a dome at the top, and either open at each side, or only at one side—in which latter case it resembles an oven; the length and height are about 5 feet, and the breadth 3 or 5. The wretched woman is laid inside on the pile of wood, over the body of her husband, to be burnt, and must soon be suffocated by the smoke. Surely this infernal rite will come to an end,

(*m*) *Suttee* is the widow who is burnt, and *sutteewár* the tomb, or altar, where the burning takes place.

though it was once gravely predicted that we could not abolish it without abolishing at the same time the British dominion in India.

Retrenchment seems to be the order of the day. The Governor-General is reducing the Native Army by 35,000 men, whereby an annual saving of 32 or 33 lákhs of rupees will be effected. A good stroke of policy this, if it can be made with safety. The effect of our late victories on the native mind is undoubtedly very great, and now perhaps is the best time to run the risk of the experiment, if that moral effect can be depended upon until the object of such retrenchment is gained. Some risk must be run, it appears, sooner or later, for our expenditure exceeds our revenue, and has done so, I believe, ever since the Affghan campaign, which was the most unfortunate crisis that ever occurred in the history of our Indian Empire. Before that time, I understand, the revenue used to exceed the expenditure by a crore and a half of rupees a year. It is to be hoped that too sanguine a reliance is not placed by our Government on the friendly professions of native states, whose friendship with us they only feel to be their own interest, so long as they cannot succeed as our enemies.

6th.—Bhárapoor Chowree, 7 miles. This being a low unhealthy spot, and the Surgeon's opinion being that the sooner we are off the ground the better, we shall deviate from our practice of halting on Sundays, and march to

7th.—Hurdwár, 13 miles. (Sunday). Divine service, but exceedingly small congregation; scarcely even an officer of the Body Guard, or of the Regiment in escort, was present: they are riding about and shooting instead. The neighbourhood abounds with tigers, and, as we have heard of one being very near us, I am going to-morrow in company with a party, who intend to search for him—an elephant having been kindly offered me. The Governor-General left the Camp yesterday, attended by his two sons, Col. Wood, Mr. Elliott, and Mr. Harvey, a civilian of Sahárunpoor, and a distinguished assailant of tigers, and took with them a light camp for a few days' sport in the jungul. To-day the skin of a very fine tiger was brought in, which they killed, after being charged by him several times.

This is a most beautiful spot at the foot of the Sewálic range of the Himálayas. We are about a mile from the Ganges, which is here as clear as crystal, and from the famous bathing-place. Krishna is said to have bathed here, and it is the only place of principal importance and peculiar sacredness for Hindoo bathing. Every year, at a certain age of the moon after the vernal equinox, the sacred spot is visited by a concourse of between 100,000 and 200,000 pilgrims. I understand that the *méla* (ⁿ) lasts from the 1st new moon to the 1st full moon after the vernal equinox. This regulation reminds us of the Easter of our Church. Every 6th year the concourse is larger than usual, and the season is called *chhota* (º) *koombh*, from the Sanskrit word *koombh*, which means the

(ⁿ) Fair, or concourse of people, for religious or commercial purposes.

(º) Little.

zodiacal sign *aquarius*. Every 12th year there is a special concourse, and the season is called *burra*(ᵖ) *koombh*, when about one million people attend; on which occasion sometimes, from the simultaneous eagerness and thronging of so vast a crowd, many are drowned. This year is the *burra koombh*. The name of the town where the Bráhmans reside, and which is close by, is Kunkul. Oh, that these poor deluded creatures could celebrate the Easter of our Church, being purified in that genuine "fountain, which has been opened for sin and uncleanness!" and what would I not give to see the same enthusiasm and ardour, with which they devote themselves to Krishna and thirst for the sacred Gunga,(ᑫ) felt and exhibited by the professing Christians of my own country, in following and serving Christ, our Passover! Missionaries sometimes attend these *mélas*, for the purpose of addressing the people; how far expedient, or how successful this may be, I know not; but if they could perform miracles, what an effect

(ᵖ) Great.   (ᑫ) Ganges.

might be expected from their preaching on such occasions! How many thousand conversions in one day! Archbishop Tillotson thought that another effusion of miraculous gifts must be vouchsafed to the Church, before the remainder of the world could be converted to the Christian Faith; but prayer is not offered for such gifts, and progress, though slow, is being made without them.

Mohun Lol is still following our Camp, though I do not ascertain for what purpose. He has lately returned from England with a pension of 1,000*l.* a year, which he has obtained from the Court of Directors in consideration, I understand, of his surrendering to them important documents connected with affairs in Affghanistan and the transactions of Sir W. MacNaghten, to whom he was Persian interpreter, or some *attaché* of the kind, and, I suppose, in consideration of some other services.

9th.—Yesterday we went out on our tiger-shooting expedition: our party consisting of 11—

too many for such an occasion. A poor villager had brought us word that a tiger had killed one of his bullocks, and that the spot was close at hand. The same man accompanied us to-day to show us the place. It was in the jungul, a thick tree-jungul, about three miles from the Camp, and there we found the remains of the carcase of the bullock, and his own strong odour assured us of the proximity of the tiger, or else of his recent departure from the spot. The thickness of the jungul made our beating it a work of great difficulty; and we were beginning to despair, when I heard the report of four shots fired. On coming up I found that accounts differed—some affirmed that one, others that two, tigers had been seen and fired at in the long grass, and had disappeared. Presently afterwards *the* beast, or *a* beast, was found again, and fired at two or three times, but disappeared. No tiger did I see from beginning to end; but some declared that their eyes had been so far satisfied. However, after beating the jungul twice over, we came away, and our expedition terminated without any prey and with much disappointment. A smaller party and more experience might have secured us better success: but only one of our gallant company understood the sport. We saw several skeletons, and two were of human beings; also, the more pleasant sight of living deer—splendid creatures, both spotted and hog-deer, níl-gais, and peafowl; and wild boars, porcupines, and monkeys varied the scene of sylvan life. The trees, the creepers, the shrubs, and all the foliage were magnificent; and none can form an exact conception of the spectacle, but they who have enjoyed the pleasure of penetrating the interior of an Indian jungul.

They say that wild elephants abound in this neighbourhood.

Here is the commencement of the Great Ganges Canal, and its length, I believe, will be about 300 miles.

To-day I went into the temple, where I beheld the most hideous idols imaginable. One was a huge cow, two were elephants, another was a black grinning monster with a human head, another blood-coloured, and there were two or three other frightful objects besides. What with the terrific spectacle of such gods of the heathen, and the thought of their being adored by millions of my fellow creatures; and the deafening noise of two large bells, or gongs, chiming, and a big drum sounding all the while, I never felt myself in a place so infernal; I shuddered with horror.

Mango-trees are very numerous here; they are just coming out into blossom, and the blossoms perfume the air delightfully; while the *cuculus Indicus* warbles among the trees in the evening, like the thrush or blackbird.

11*th*.—The Governor-General returned to-day, much pleased with his successful sport. They killed two tigers, one of them having charged his Lordship's elephant twice, and also a bear. Bears, I understand, are not often found in the plains.

12*th*.—The Governor-General has gone with a light camp to Dehra-dhoon. Thence his Lordship intends to proceed to Mussooree, and so to Simla. We, who remain with the heavy camp, shall march to Umballa, and thence proceed to Simla. It is very warm now in the day-time. Our march to-day has been 13 miles, to *Dowlutpoor*.

13*th*. — *Secundrapoor*, 13 miles. A villager having reported that a tiger was about two miles from the camp, ten of us went out on elephants, beat the jungul, which consisted only of bushes and brambles, through and through, but returned with downcast looks, and the conviction that the intelligence must have been a false alarm, though the villagers persisted in declaring that they had heard the beast roaring in that very place last night and this morning.

The feats of elephants are wonderful; they will go over anything, and up and down most awkward declivities at an angle of 45°, and through the thickest jungul of thorns, feeling their way, when suspicious, and breaking down every obstacle. One of ours, to-day, having trod upon a large

DEPARTURE FROM LAHORE, ETC. 209

thorn, stopped, and tried to extricate it with his trunk; but he could not succeed, and the Mahout was obliged to extract it for him, while the poor creature roared with pain.

It appears that, notwithstanding all the measures of retrenchment which our Government are adopting, the expenditure of India exceeds the revenue by 21 lakhs, besides the amount of the 5 per cent. interest for the money they are borrowing. See, for explanation of this, the *Delhi Gazette* of 10th March, 1847.

Every day since we left Hurdwár we have met on the road numbers of pilgrims, men, women and children, proceeding thither.

14*th*. — *Sahárunpoor*, 13 miles. (Sunday). — Divine Service, as usual; but only one person belonging to the Station attended, though all must have known of the Service. It is a small Civil Station, of which Mr. Harvey, the great tiger hunter, is Judge; and being an ecclesiastical out-station of Meerut, it is visited twice a year by the chaplains of that station. But, though the

P

residents of these minor stations are always ready to complain of their want of the public means of grace, yet when a rare opportunity like the present occurs, and these means *are* available, what a proof do they give of their sincerity! There has been no necessity for our marching to-day; and, understanding that arrangements have been made for our marching into Umballa next Sunday, I remonstrated, and expressed a hope to Colonel Stuart that it might not be so, unless some absolute necessity existed; in consequence of this, though it gave offence, I am glad to hear that the arrangement has been altered.

15th.—There is a botanical garden here, supported by Government, and Dr. Jamieson is the superintendent of it. The garden is beautifully laid out, and full of rare trees and plants. It is useful as well as ornamental, for it produces various vegetables, and supplies other places with seeds of flowers and plants. What an advantage it were to large stations, if such gardens could be attached to them! But the expense would be too great: in this one garden, 80 *málees*(r) are employed. I saw, in a flower-pot, a small tea-plant, a specimen from Dehra-dhoon. The tea plantation there, I believe, is likely to answer. The Governor-General has gone to see it, and Dr. Jamieson meets him there. A mahogany-tree is another of the rarities here. I do not know whether the garden is to be called zoological as well as botanical; but part of it is occupied by a small menagerie, with six or seven tenants.

16*th.*—*Chilkána*, 10 miles.

17*th.*—*Booriah*, 10 miles. We crossed the Jumna on our way by a bridge of boats. This place is disfigured by a cluster of old *sutteewárs*. A Ránee resides here; and a pretty piece of ground, skirted by the river Jumna, reminds one of an English park. The trees of the park are all mangoes, and our encampment is in a mango-grove.

18*th.*—*Mustaphebád*, 13½ miles.

(r) Gardeners.

19th.—Freefulla, 14 miles. Weather very warm now.

20th.—Umballa, 8 miles. Looks just as it did last year, a straggling dreary station; roads unformed; the only addition, some artillery barracks; the same building still used as a church—a place like a barn—and no better edifice in progress.

I am glad to meet here an old acquaintance, who has obtained a respectable situation, after much affliction and difficulty, having resigned the Oudh service (military) in disgust, the moral wretchedness of which service and the abominations of Lucknow I remember his relating to me at Cánpoor: I rejoice in his comparative comfort and prosperity, though certainly Rs. 200 a month is but very little for a large family; but I rejoice more in his humble and modest piety.

21st.—(Sunday.)—Divine Service in tent as usual. Congregation very thin, partly in consequence of the reduction of our Camp; but two of the members of the Camp never attend, and only one of the Aide-de-Camps is a regular attendant. I hear that no Service is held to-day in the Station-Church, one of the Chaplains being ill and the other having gone with his family to Simla. I was not requested by the resident Chaplain to officiate for him; and only one family belonging to the station and one non-commissioned officer came to join in our Service here.

I am glad to find that a Chaplain has at last been appointed to Lahore. The Roman Catholic Priest there has set us an example of zeal and expedition, and is already building a chapel.

Atmosphere extremely close all day.

22nd.—*Dubán*, 13 miles. Air this morning quite suffocating.

23rd.—*Munnamájra*, 13 miles. Air this morning delightfully cooled by a breeze from the hills. We hear that snow is still lying about Simla, three or four feet deep in some places, and that this year the fall has been heavy. Part of the country we have passed through to-day has a Bengálee appearance, being covered with rice-fields and palm-trees. But again the proximity and view of the hills dismiss all thoughts of Bengál. This place is in the territory of the Rájah of Putteeála, who is holding a great méla here to-day.

Thermometer at 2 P.M. 94°.

24th.—Kalka, 11 miles. Very hot: difficult to say whether roasting, boiling, stewing, or baking, be the most appropriate term to express the process we are undergoing. However, our tabernacle-life for the present has now come to an end; and, interesting and healthful as our tour has been, still the houses and snow and rhododendrons of Simla will· be a pleasant and refreshing change.

And such is the mortal life of Christians—of those, I mean, who are truly Christians. Their bodies are tabernacles;[*] their days are movement and change; they are strangers and pilgrims

[*] 2 Cor. v. 1, 4. 1 Pet. i. 13, 14.

on the earth; here they have no continuing city, no certain resting-place; and they desire a better country, that is, a heavenly, and look for the dissolution of these tabernacles (*f*) and for a city that hath foundations.

(*f*) 2 Cor. v. 1, 4.   1 Pet. i. 13, 14.

www.ingramcontent.com/pod-product-compliance
Lightning Source LLC
Chambersburg PA
CBHW070656100426
42735CB00039B/2167